Collins | English for Exams

WRITING FOR IELTS

Published by Collins
An imprint of HarperCollins Publishers
Westerhill Road
Bishopbriggs
Glasgow
G64 2QT

Second edition 2019

10 9 8 7 6 5 4 3 2 1

ISBN 978-0-00-836753-4

www.collinselt.com

A catalogue record for this book is available from the British
Library.

If you would like to comment on any aspect of this book,
please contact us at the given address or online.
E-mail: dictionaries@harpercollins.co.uk

  facebook.com/collinselt

@CollinsELT

Author: Anneli Williams
Series editor: Matthew Duffy
For the Publisher: Lisa Todd and Kerry Ferguson
Typesetter: Jouve, India
Printer: Martins, UK
Photo credits: p80 (right): © Anton_Ivanov / Shutterstock.
All other images from Shutterstock.
Cover illustration: © Maria Herbert-Liew 2019
Sample IELTS Writing answer sheets (pages 143–4): Reproduced
with permission of Cambridge Assessment English
© UCLES 2019

All exam-style questions and sample answers in this title were
written by the author.

About the author
Anneli Williams has taught English for Academic Purposes at the
University of Glasgow for over 24 years, developing extensive
experience preparing students for the IELTS examination as well
as for academic study within university settings.

Author's acknowledgements
I would like to thank my family, especially my partner Steven
and my daughter Ruby, for their support and patience. I would
also like to thank series editor Matthew Duffy for his feedback
and advice, always spot-on and graciously delivered, and finally
Kerry Ferguson and Lisa Todd at HarperCollins for taking this
project forward.

MIX
Paper from
responsible sources
FSC™ C007454

FSC
www.fsc.org

This book is produced from independently
certified FSC™ paper to ensure responsible
forest management.

For more information visit:
www.harpercollins.co.uk/green

Contents

Introduction

Who is this book for?

Writing for IELTS will prepare you for the IELTS Writing test whether you are taking the test for the first time, or re-sitting the test. It has been written for learners with band score 5–5.5 who are trying to achieve band score 6.5 or higher.

The structured approach, comprehensive answer key and model answers have been designed so that you can use the materials to study on your own. However, the book can also be used as a supplementary writing skills course for IELTS preparation classes. The book provides enough material for approximately 50 hours of classroom time.

Content

Writing for IELTS is divided into 12 units. Each unit focuses on a topic area that you are likely to encounter in the IELTS Writing test. This helps you to build up a bank of vocabulary and ideas related to a variety of the topics.

Units 1–11 cover the key stages of the writing process: everything from analysing the task to proof-reading a completed response. Every exercise is relevant to the exam. The aims listed at the start of each unit specify the key skills, techniques and language covered in the unit. You work towards Unit 12, which provides a final practice IELTS Writing test.

Additionally, the book provides exam strategies telling you what to expect and how best to succeed in the exam. *Exam information* is presented in clear, easy-to-read boxes. *Exam tips* in each unit highlight essential exam techniques and can be rapidly reviewed at a glance.

There are also *Watch Out!* boxes that will help you avoid common errors made in the exam. Finally, the *Exam tutor* at the end of each unit gives you the opportunity to revise and consolidate the exam skills you have studied.

Unit structure

Each of the first 11 units is divided into three parts.

Part 1 Language development introduces vocabulary related to the topic as well as some of the most common academic words and expressions needed for the writing functions covered in the unit. A range of exercises gives you the opportunity to use the vocabulary in a variety of contexts. These exercises also build awareness of the patterns in words and language items. The vocabulary is presented using Collins COBUILD dictionary definitions.

Part 2 Exam skills provides step-by-step exercises and guidance on the key stages of the writing process. There are guided questions and worked examples to show you what an effective IELTS Writing response looks like. Useful expressions and grammatical forms are highlighted, and there are exercises that help you develop good range and accuracy in your writing. You are encouraged to apply what you have learnt, while at the same time writing your own responses to task questions. *Exam information* and *Exam tips* show you how to approach each task type and will help you develop successful test-taking strategies.

Part 3 Exam practice provides exam practice questions for Task 1 and Task 2 in a format that follows the actual exam. You can use this as a means of assessing your readiness for the actual exam. There is also an *Exam tutor* checklist after the exam practice that will help you revise and consolidate key points to improve your writing.

Answer key

A comprehensive answer key is provided for all sections of the book, including recommended answers and explanations for more open-ended writing tasks. There are model answers for all of the writing questions. For one of the practice exam questions in each unit, two model answers are given – one of them annotated. This shows you that a variety of approaches to each writing task can be taken.

Using the book for self-study

If you are new to IELTS, we recommend that you work systematically through the 12 units in order to benefit from its progressive structure. If you are a more experienced learner, you can use the aims listed at the start of each unit to select the most useful exercises.

Each unit contains between three to four hours of self-study material. Having access to someone who can provide informed feedback on the writing practice exercises is an advantage. However, you can still learn a lot working alone, or with a study partner willing to give and receive peer feedback.

Part 1: Language development

Ideally, you should begin each unit by working through the *Part 1: Language development* exercises. Try to answer the questions without looking at a dictionary in order to develop the skill of inferring the meaning of unfamiliar words from context.

Part 2: Exam skills

Work through the *Part 2: Exam skills* from beginning to end. It is important to study the *Exam information* and *Exam tips* about each of the question types, so that you become familiar with how to approach the different writing tasks in the exam. Doing this will also help you develop more general writing skills. The grammar points covered should be thoroughly mastered so that during the actual exam you can focus on the higher order skills of planning and effectively communicating your response.

Part 3: Exam practice

This section contains exam practice with timed questions. This gives you the opportunity to practise writing to a time limit. If you find this difficult at first, you could focus first on writing a high-quality response of the correct length. Then you could start to reduce the time allowed gradually until you are able to write an acceptable answer within the time limit. Model answers should be studied to identify the underlying approach and effect on the reader. Try not to memorise essays or reports or to attempt to fit a pre-existing response around another exam question. If you work systematically through the book, you should develop the skills and language to effectively express your own responses to unseen exam questions on the day.

Unit 12 Practice exam

This is a complete practice Writing exam. This unit should be done under exam conditions.

Using the book in the classroom

If you are a teacher, you can use *Writing for IELTS* either as your main IELTS coursebook or as a supplementary course. Detailed teacher's notes for each unit are available at: www.collinselt.com/teachielts.

The International English Language Testing System (IELTS) test

IELTS is jointly managed by the British Council, Cambridge ESOL Examinations and IDP Education, Australia. There are two versions of the test:

- Academic
- General Training

Academic is for students wishing to study at undergraduate or postgraduate levels in an English-medium environment.

General Training is for people who wish to migrate to an English-speaking country. This book is primarily for students taking the Academic version.

The test

There are four modules:

Listening	30 minutes, plus 10 minutes for transferring answers to the answer sheet. NB: the audio is heard *only once*. Approx. 10 questions per section Section 1: two speakers discuss a social situation Section 2: one speaker talks about a non-academic topic Section 3: up to four speakers discuss an educational project Section 4: one speaker gives a talk of general academic interest
Reading	60 minutes 3 texts, taken from authentic sources, on general, academic topics. They may contain diagrams, charts, etc. 40 questions: may include multiple choice, sentence completion, completing a diagram, graph or chart, choosing headings, yes/no, true/false questions, classification and matching exercises.
Writing	Task 1: 20 minutes: description of a table, chart, graph or diagram (150 words minimum) Task 2: 40 minutes: an essay in response to an argument or problem (250 words minimum)
Speaking	11–14 minutes A three-part face-to-face oral interview with an examiner. The interview is recorded. Part 1: introductions and general questions (4–5 mins) Part 2: individual long turn (3–4 mins) – the candidate is given a task, has one minute to prepare, then talks for 1–2 minutes, with some questions from the examiner. Part 3: two-way discussion (4–5 mins): the examiner asks further questions on the topic from Part 2, and gives the candidate the opportunity to discuss more abstract issues or ideas.
Timetabling	Listening, Reading and Writing must be taken on the same day, and in the order listed above. Speaking can be taken up to 7 days before or after the other modules.
Scoring	Each section is given a band score. The average of the four scores produces the Overall Band Score. You do not pass or fail IELTS; you receive a score.

IELTS and the Common European Framework of Reference

The CEFR shows the level of the learner and is used for many English as a Foreign Language examinations. The table below shows the approximate CEFR level and the equivalent IELTS Overall Band Score:

CEFR description	CEFR level	IELTS Band Score
Proficient user (Advanced)	C2 C1	9 7–8
Independent user (Intermediate – Upper Intermediate)	B2 B1	5–6.5 4–5

This table contains the general descriptors for the band scores 1–9:

IELTS Band Scores		
9	Expert user	Has fully operational command of the language: appropriate, accurate and fluent with complete understanding.
8	Very good user	Has fully operational command of the language, with only occasional unsystematic inaccuracies and inappropriacies. Misunderstandings may occur in unfamiliar situations. Handles complex detailed argumentation well.
7	Good user	Has operational command of the language, though with occasional inaccuracies, inappropriacies and misunderstandings in some situations. Generally handles complex language well and understands detailed reasoning.
6	Competent user	Has generally effective command of the language despite some inaccuracies, inappropriacies and misunderstandings. Can use and understand fairly complex language, particularly in familiar situations.
5	Modest user	Has partial command of the language, coping with overall meaning in most situations, though is likely to make many mistakes. Should be able to handle basic communication in own field.
4	Limited user	Basic competence is limited to familiar situations. Has frequent problems in understanding and expression. Is not able to use complex language.
3	Extremely limited user	Conveys and understands only general meaning in very familiar situations. Frequent breakdowns in communication occur.
2	Intermittent user	No real communication is possible except for the most basic information using isolated words or short formulae in familiar situations and to meet immediate needs. Has great difficulty understanding spoken and written English.
1	Non user	Essentially has no ability to use the language beyond possibly a few isolated words.
0	Did not attempt the test	No assessable information provided.

Marking

The Listening and Reading papers have 40 items, each worth one mark if correctly answered. Here are some examples of how marks are translated into band scores:

Listening:
16 out of 40 correct answers:	band score 5
23 out of 40 correct answers:	band score 6
30 out of 40 correct answers:	band score 7

Reading:
15 out of 40 correct answers:	band score 5
23 out of 40 correct answers:	band score 6
30 out of 40 correct answers:	band score 7

Writing and Speaking are marked according to performance descriptors.

Writing: examiners award a band score for each of four areas with equal weighting:

- Task achievement (Task 1)
- Task response (Task 2)
- Coherence and cohesion
- Lexical resource and grammatical range and accuracy

Speaking: examiners award a band score for each of four areas with equal weighting:

- Fluency and coherence
- Lexical resource
- Grammatical range
- Accuracy and pronunciation

For full details of how the examination is scored and marked, go to: www.ielts.org

1 Gender roles

Part 1: Language development

Describing character traits

Women are more suitable for caring professions like nursing.

My brothers are typical boys – always arguing about who's the boss.

Boys like to fight, but girls almost always do as they're told.

You have to be nice to girls because they get upset so easily.

1   Read the comments above and decide which words a-h the speakers associate with males or with females. Write M for males and F for females.

   a   aggressive ____   d   compliant ____   g   vulnerable ____
   b   authoritative ____   e   gentle ____   h   confident ____
   c   competitive ____   f   strong ____

2   Complete sentences 1–6 with the noun form (singular or plural) of the adjectives in brackets.

   Boys are not usually encouraged to show <u>vulnerability</u>. (vulnerable)

   1   Many people believe that men and women have different _____. (strong)
   2   _____ is not an exclusively feminine characteristic. (gentle)
   3   It is sometimes argued that women do not achieve their goals because they lack _____. (confident)
   4   Some people have difficulty working with female _____ figures. (authoritative)

> ### 💡 Exam tip
> In Task 2, you often have to write about ideas and issues rather than about individual people. A knowledge of abstract nouns will help you write in an academic way, e.g. *Aggression is commonly considered a masculine trait.*

5 While men tend to be praised for leadership, women are often praised for _____. (compliant)

6 _____ is commonly associated with masculinity. (competitive)

! Watch out

Make sure you use the correct word class (verb, noun, adjective or adverb).

Describing figures and tables

i Exam information: Summarising information

In Writing Task 1, you often have to summarise information presented in a visual form. You should familiarise yourself with the different types of visual prompts and the kind of information they represent.

3 Complete the descriptions 1–8 of the figures below with the words a–f. (Words can be used more than once).

a column
b features
c axis

d row
e stage
f segment

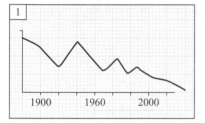

A **line graph** typically illustrates trends. Here the horizontal (1) _____ represents time and the vertical (2) _____ represents the characteristic that changes over time.

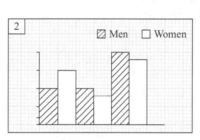

A **bar chart** is often used to make comparisons between categories of items. Each (3) _____ represents one category.

A **pie chart** shows how a whole is composed of parts. Each (4) _____ indicates a percentage of the whole.

A **table** is often used to categorise data when precise figures are needed. This example contains three (5) _____ and four (6) _____ of numbers.

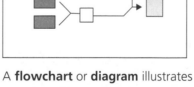

A **flowchart** or **diagram** illustrates a process. Here each box represents one (7) _____ in the process.

A **map** illustrates the (8) _____ of a location, such as roads, bridges and railway lines.

Part 2: Exam skills

Task 1: Understanding the task

> ### *i* Exam information: Form completion (1)
> In Writing Task 1, you have to identify and describe the key information presented in one or more graphs, charts, or diagrams. You should include a short introduction, one to three body paragraphs and a brief concluding paragraph (optional).

1 Read the Task 1 instructions below and answer questions 1–4.

WRITING TASK 1

You should spend about 20 minutes on this task.

The chart below shows the numbers of male and female research students studying six science-related subjects at a UK university in 2019.

Summarise the information by selecting and reporting the main features, and make comparisons where relevant.

Write at least 150 words.

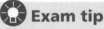

> ### 🔆 Exam tip
> You will be assessed and marked on 'task achievement'. This means you must understand and follow the instructions carefully.

1 How long should you spend on this task?
2 How many words do you need to write?
3 Will you score higher marks if you include all the information in the chart?
4 Are you expected to give your opinion about the information?

> ### 🔆 Exam tip
> There is no one correct answer to a writing task. However, there are some common ways of organising your response and the type of information included.

Overview of task

2 Read the sample answer below and answer questions 1–6.

1 What information does the introduction contain?

_____

_____

2 What is the main focus of the first body paragraph?

_____

_____

3 What is the main focus of the second body paragraph?

_____

_____

4 What is the purpose of the first sentence in each of the body paragraphs?

_____

_____

5 What is the purpose of the second and third sentences in each body paragraph?

_____

_____

6 What is the purpose of the conclusion?

_____

_____

The chart shows the gender distribution of students doing scientific research across a range of disciplines at a UK university in 2019.

Male students made up a large proportion of the student group in subjects related to the study of objects and materials: physics, astronomy, and geology. The gender gap was particularly large in the field of physics, where there were five times as many male students as female students.

Women students outnumbered male students in subjects related to the study of living things: biology, medicine, and veterinary medicine. In biology, there were significantly more women (approximately 230) than men (approximately 180). This was also true of medicine, and especially veterinary medicine, where there were twice as many female research students as male research students.

Overall, the chart shows that at this university there were differences in the type of scientific research undertaken by male and female students.

☀ Exam tip

Do not describe all of the information in the figure. The purpose of Task 1 is to test your ability to summarise the key information and to select appropriate examples to support your key observations.

Task 2: Understanding the task

ℹ Exam information: Writing solutions to problems

In Writing Task 2, you have to write an essay of four to six paragraphs in answer to a question. The question will ask you to evaluate or present an idea or solution to a problem. Your aim should be to present a strong argument, supported by evidence.

3 Read the Task 2 instructions below and complete statements 1–4 by circling a or b.

> **WRITING TASK 2**
>
> You should spend about 40 minutes on this task.
>
> Write about the following topic:
>
> In spite of the many advances, women have made in education and employment, they continue to be at a disadvantage when it comes to pay and promotion. In your view, what should be done to promote equality of opportunity for men and women in the workplace?
>
> Give reasons for your answer and include any relevant examples from your own knowledge or experience.
>
> Write at least 250 words.

1 You should spend:
   a   more time on Task 2 than on Task 1.
   b   the same amount of time on Task 2 and Task 1.

2 In your response you should mainly:
   a   explain why women are at a disadvantage.
   b   suggest solutions to the problem of inequality in the workplace.

3 To support your opinion, you should:
   a   give reasons and examples.
   b   give reasons or examples.

4 You have to write:
   a   more than 250 words.
   b   fewer than 250 words.

💡 Exam tip

Task 2 counts for more of your final mark than Task 1. You should spend more time writing your Task 2 response.

Overview of task

4 Read the sample answer on page 13 and the explanatory comments in the boxes. Complete the boxes 1–5 by adding the comments a–e.

   a   an example
   b   summary of your main points
   c   a better solution
   d   an acknowledgement that there are difficulties
   e   advantage of this solution

Description of the situation and problem	In many parts of the world, there is now greater equality between working men and women. Nevertheless, women still tend to earn less and enjoy fewer promotions than men. Some would argue that this situation will correct itself over time. However, in my view, there is much that can be done to address the problem constructively.

An opposing opinion

Your opinion and plan

One possible approach would be for governments to force employers to promote the same numbers of men and women and to pay them the same salaries. This would certainly tackle the problem quickly. However, measures like this would probably be seen as excessive and difficult to enforce.

One possible but not ideal solution

An advantage of this solution

A disadvantage of this solution

A more feasible approach would be for governments themselves to take the lead by ensuring that their male and female employees earn the same for equivalent work and that women are promoted fairly. This would help to establish gender equality as a norm and set a good example for companies in the private sector. Countries, such as Sweden and Iceland, which have done this are often regarded by others as socially-advanced models.

1 _____

An advantage of this solution

2 _____

Another solution

To further encourage equality, companies could be required to publish figures on the rank and average earnings of men and women in their workforce. Evidence of large inequalities would create a bad impression. In order to avoid bad publicity, companies might consider it worthwhile to pay fairer wages and promote more women to management positions.

3 _____

4 _____

It is true that the problem of gender inequality in the workplace will probably not be solved quickly. However, that is not a reason to avoid taking action. Governments can encourage change by showing the way forward and taking advantage of the need for companies to present themselves as fair and reasonable.

Restatement of your opinion

5 _____

5 Read the text again and answer questions 1–5.

1 How long is the introduction?
2 How many body paragraphs are there?
3 How many main points are there?
4 In what order are solutions discussed?
5 What is the main purpose of the conclusion?

☀ Exam tip

Spend six to seven minutes on analysing the question, thinking of ideas, and making a plan. Spend about 30 minutes writing your essay, and three to four minutes checking your essay for mistakes.

There are often four categories of Task 2 questions (a–d below). The question type will help you decide on how you plan and write your essay. Each type requires you to do something different.

Task 2 question types	Examples
a Propose one or more solutions to a problem	*How can the problem of inequality in the workplace best be addressed?*
b Evaluate a solution to a problem	*Many people believe that boys and girls learn better when they are educated separately. What is your view on this practice?*
c Provide an explanation or prediction	*What do you see as the main reasons for gender inequality in the workplace?*
d Evaluate an idea or belief	*Many people maintain that boys are naturally more aggressive than girls. To what extent do you agree with this view?*

6 Read the essay questions 1–4 below and indicate the type of essay (a–d) you need to write. (See the Exam Information box above.) Underline the words in the essay question that helped you decide.

1   Why do you think women generally hold fewer positions of power?

2   In many parts of the world, unemployment among men is rising whilst the number of positions in jobs traditionally held by women is increasing. Do you think that women will overtake men as the main wage earners?

3   To what extent should governments intervene in the labour market to ensure that men and women are paid the same amount for equivalent work?

4   Although there has been a large increase in the numbers of women who go out to work, women continue to do a disproportionate amount of housework and childcare. What can be done to promote greater equality between men and women within the home?

Part 3: Exam practice

WRITING TASK 1: Describe a bar chart

You should spend about 20 minutes on this task. Write at least 150 words.

The chart shows the percentage of male and female teachers in six different types of educational setting in the UK in 2019. Summarise the information by selecting and reporting the main features, and make comparisons where relevant.

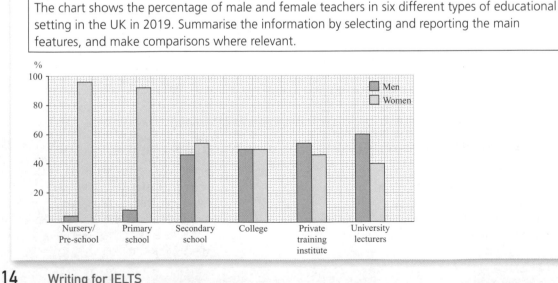

WRITING TASK 2: Write an essay evaluating a belief

You should spend about 40 minutes on this task. Write about the following topic:

Women and men are commonly seen as having different strengths and weaknesses. Is it right to exclude males or females from certain professions because of their gender?

Give reasons for your answer and include any relevant examples from your own knowledge or experience.

Write at least 250 words.

🎓 Exam tutor

1 How many words should you write for each Writing task?

2 When writing a Task 1 summary, should you include as much detailed information as possible?

3 When writing a Task 2 essay, should you focus on your personal opinions and experiences?

4 Which task should you spend more time writing?

5 What are the four main types of Task 2 questions?

2 Diet and nutrition

Language development | Expressions related to food and diet; Describing line graphs; Time expressions related to line graphs
Exam skills | Task 1: Structuring a line graph response; Writing an introduction and conclusion; Task 2: Taking a stance on an issue; Generating ideas for your essay
Exam practice | Task 1: Describe a line graph; Task 2: Write an essay evaluating an idea

Part 1: Language development

Expressions related to food and diet

Exam tip

One of the criteria used to mark your writing is 'lexical resource'. That means having a good knowledge of vocabulary, such as collocations, and how to use it.

1 Match the expressions 1–10 with the correct definitions a–j.

1	organic food	a	fruit and vegetables available at particular times of the year
2	dietary supplement	b	a basic food that is regularly eaten
3	fast food	c	food that needs little preparation and can be used at any time
4	food security	d	a diet without meat or fish
5	seasonal produce	e	a diet that provides all of the nutrients required
6	convenience food	f	the state of having reliable access to food
7	vegetarian diet	g	tablets or foods taken to improve nutrition
8	health consciousness	h	food grown without artificial fertilizers or pesticides
9	staple food	i	food that can be obtained quickly from a restaurant
10	balanced diet	j	having an active interest in one's health

Describing line graphs

2 Match expressions a–i with the part of the graph it best describes.

a peaked
b fluctuated
c rose steadily
d fell sharply
e levelled off
f decreased gradually
g declined rapidly
h reached its lowest point
i increased moderately

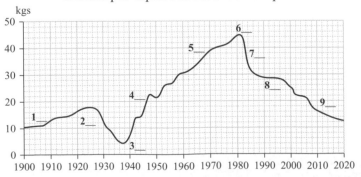

Annual per capita red meat consumption

🔆 Exam tip

When describing line graphs, you can use a wider range of sentence patterns.
1 verb + adverb, e.g. *Meat consumption dipped slightly.*
2 *There + to be +* adjective + noun (+*in*), e.g. *There was a slight dip in meat consumption.*

3 Sentences 1–5 describe the graph in Exercise 2 on page 16. Re-write each sentence using *there + to be* + adjective + noun (+ *in*).

Consumption dipped slightly. – There was a slight dip in consumption.

1 Annual consumption of red meat increased moderately. _____
2 It then declined rapidly. _____
3 Meat consumption rose steadily. _____
4 It fell sharply again. _____
5 The annual consumption of red meat per person decreased gradually. _____

Time expressions related to line graphs

4 Read the line graph description below. Underline the time expressions and circle the phrases that give specific figures.

> Between 1918 and 1922, there was a moderate increase in the consumption of red meat from a low of 12 kgs to a high of 18 kgs per person. During the following ten-year period, it declined rapidly to its lowest point of just over 5 kgs. From 1950 to 1980, meat consumption rose steadily, reaching its highest point at 45 kgs. In 1980, it fell sharply again to approximately 30 kgs. From 1990 onwards, consumption of red meat per person decreased gradually by approximately 60 percent.

5 Write a paragraph describing the graph below. Use a mix of sentence patterns and include information about the time frame and specific figures from the graph.

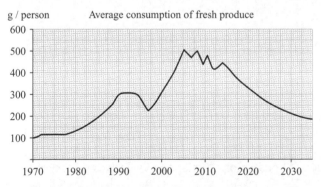

🔆 Exam tip

Adding specific information from the graph will make your summary more precise. A common pattern to describe change over time is:

Time frame + main clause + specific figures

From 1900 to 1915, consumption dipped slightly from 15 kgs to 12 kgs.

Part 2: Exam skills

Task 1: Structuring a line graph response

> ### ℹ Exam information: Task 1 introductions and conclusions
> A Task 1 introduction typically begins with statements about the kind of information shown in the visual prompt.
> The conclusion normally gives a summary of the most significant information or message from the prompt.

Writing an introduction and conclusion

Watch out

Make sure you use the right units of measurement, e.g. numbers, percentages, units of 1000, etc. Before you start writing, look carefully at how the axes of the graph are labelled.

1 Choose the best introductory sentence a–c for the graph below about food insecurity.

    a The graph shows the number of UK households which experienced food insecurity and severe food insecurity between 2000 and 2020.

    b The graph shows the percentage of UK households which experienced food security and the percentage of those which did not experience food security.

    c The graph shows changes in the overall percentage of UK households which did not have reliable access to food as well as those which experienced very low food security over a twenty-year period.

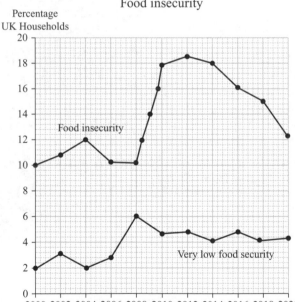

Food insecurity

2 Choose the best conclusion a–c for the graph in Exercise 1.

    a Following a sharp rise in 2006, the percentage of households experiencing very low food security doubled over the twenty-year period.

    b Food insecurity grew most significantly between 2006 and 2010. While food insecurity overall declined from 2014, the percentage of households most severely affected by food insecurity remained roughly the same over the final six-year period.

    c Overall food insecurity rose slightly, fell in 2004, then rose again to 16 percent then fell again to 12 percent. Very low food security started at three percent, stayed roughly the same for six years, then rose slightly to six percent, then stayed at roughly four percent until 2020.

3 Write two main paragraphs for the graph in Exercise 1 on page 18. Include information about the time frame and specific figures from the graph where required. Each paragraph should be about 50 words long.

Paragraph 1: Describe the line representing overall food insecurity using the sentence pattern: *there be* + adjective + noun (+ *in*).

Paragraph 2: Describe the line representing very low food security using the sentence pattern: verb + adverb.

Exam tip

If the visual prompt contains two or more graphs, your summary should indicate the connection between them. For example, you should state whether the trends shown are broadly similar or different.

Task 2: Taking a stance on an issue

i Exam information: Presenting your opinion

In order to present a strong argument, you should first decide what your opinion, or 'stance', is in relation to the issue in the question. When you write your essay, you must give reasons, or 'evidence', for your stance. You can show that you have 'tested' your opinion by comparing it with at least one other opinion.

4 Mark statements 1–5 according to how closely they represent your opinion: SA (Strongly agree), A (agree), D (disagree), SD (strongly disagree).

1 *We should return to more natural methods of food production, such as organic farming, even if this means that we produce food less efficiently.*

2 *In order to improve public health, governments should require food manufacturers to add nutrients to their products.*

3 *The problem of rising levels of obesity in many parts of the world is mainly due to people's lack of knowledge about food and nutrition.*

4 *Fast food is generally unhealthy, so governments should regulate the fast food industry in the same way that they regulate the alcohol and tobacco industries.*

5 *Convenience food will become increasingly prevalent and eventually replace traditional foods and traditional methods of food preparation.*

5 Read the opinions below and the reasons a–g. Indicate which reasons support each opinion by writing letters a–g in the spaces provided. The first one has been done for you.

1 Some people strongly agree that we should return to more natural methods of food production, such as organic farming, even if this means that we produce food less efficiently. They believe this because: _c_ , ___ , ___

2 Other people strongly disagree that we should return to more natural methods of food production, such as organic farming, even if this means that we produce food less efficiently. They believe this because:___ , ___ , ___ , ___

Reasons

a More people will need to be employed on farms, and fewer people will be available to do work that will help the country develop economically.

b Producing food less efficiently could lead to food shortages.

c It is better for the environment to produce food using fewer chemicals such as pesticides and herbicides.

d Organically produced food is no more nutritious than food produced using pesticides and artificial fertilisers.

e Naturally produced food tastes better than food produced using more artificial methods.

f Food that has been produced without preservatives is less likely to stay fresh, so more food may be wasted.

g Man-made chemicals used in modern methods of food production could be harmful to human health.

Generating ideas for your essay

6 Read the essay questions 1 and 2 and complete Templates A and B with the missing information a–h below.

1 What can governments do to encourage children to eat a healthier diet?

Template A: Propose one or more solutions to a problem

	What are the possible solutions?	What specific action can be taken?	What are the positive consequences?	What are the drawbacks?
1	Regulate the food industry	Require food producers to fortify their products with vitamins	1 _____	This would be unpopular and expensive for food producers
2	Regulate school meals	2 _____	Children would have at least one healthy meal per day	This would not stop children from bringing unhealthy packed lunches or going out for lunch to fast food outlets
3	3 _____	Require schools to teach children to cook healthy foods	Children can take pride in their learning and transfer these skills to the home	4 _____

a Schools may not have the facilities to teach cooking
b Children would eat healthier food without having to change their habits
c Require schools to provide only healthy food and drink at lunchtime
d Educate children about healthy eating

2 Should the government regulate the fast food industry in the same way that it regulates the drug, alcohol and tobacco industries?

Template B: Evaluate the solution

	What are the possible solutions?	What specific action can be taken?	What are the positive consequences?	What are the drawbacks?
1	**Solution in the question:** Regulate the fast food industry like drug, alcohol and tobacco industries	Restrict opening hours. Restrict location, e.g. not near schools	Send a clear signal that fast food is bad for health 5 _____	This would not stop people cooking and eating unhealthy food at home 6 _____
2	**Alternative solution:** Public health campaign explaining the dangers of eating too much fast food	Television advertising showing long-term consequences of an unhealthy diet	Help people change their eating habits fundamentally 7 _____	People could ignore government advice 8 _____

e Reduces people's access to unhealthy foods
f Effectiveness of public health campaigns can be difficult to measure
g Allows freedom of choice
h Too much government interference is unpopular with business and bad for the economy

7 Read the essay questions 1 and 2 and use your own ideas to complete Templates C and D.

> **1** Dieting to lose weight has become increasingly common in the developed world. Why do you think people nowadays are so concerned with body shape and size?

Template C: Provide an explanation or prediction

	What are your ideas?	What is the evidence for?	What is the evidence against?
1	Advertisements encourage people to value slim figures	Advertisements often show desirable consumer products alongside slim models	Advertisers wouldn't use slim models unless the public already had a favourable view of them
2	People associate slimness with positive character traits	People who do not eat too much are seen as having good self-control	1 _____ _____ _____
3	2 _____ _____ _____	3 _____ _____	If people diet too much, they may become malnourished

> **2** Unhealthy eating habits are due to a lack of knowledge about healthy eating. To what extent do you agree with the statement above?

Template D: Evaluate an idea or belief

What are the ideas?	What is the evidence for?	What is the evidence against?
Idea in the question: Unhealthy eating habits are due to lack of knowledge about healthy eating	4 _____ _____ _____	5 _____ _____ _____
Alternative idea: 6 _____ _____ _____	7 _____ _____ _____	8 _____ _____ _____

Part 3: Exam practice

WRITING TASK 1: Describe a line graph

You should spend about 20 minutes on this task. Write at least 150 words.

> The graph shows the number of UK adolescents following a vegetarian diet.
> Summarise the information by selecting and reporting the main features.

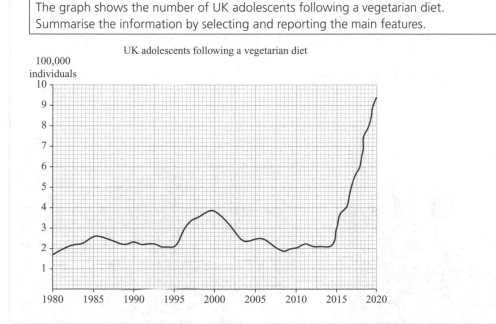

WRITING TASK 2: Write an essay evaluating an idea

You should spend about 40 minutes on this task. Write about the following topic:

> Convenience foods will become increasingly prevalent and eventually replace traditional foods and
> traditional methods of food preparation. To what extent do you agree or disagree with this opinion?

**Give reasons for your answer and include any relevant examples from your own knowledge or
experience. Write at least 250 words.**

🎓 Exam tutor

1 Which two sentence patterns are commonly used to describe line graphs?

2 What other information is commonly included in sentences describing a line graph?

3 How do Task 1 summaries typically begin and end?

4 In a Task 2 essay, is it acceptable to discuss more than one opinion?

5 In a Task 2 essay, is it acceptable to include points against your own opinion?

3 Educational goals

Language development | College and university subjects; Collocations related to education; Expressing quantity
Exam skills | Task 1: Comparing and contrasting information; Describing information in bar charts; Task 2: Selecting and organising ideas; Writing an essay outline
Exam practice | Task 1: Describe a bar chart; Task 2: Write an essay evaluating an idea

Part 1: Language development

College and university subjects

1 Categorise the subjects below into three groups: Arts and Humanities (AH), Social Sciences (SS) or Science and Technology (ST)

mathematics ___	philosophy ___	chemistry ___	business studies ___
media studies ___	English literature ___	sociology ___	biology ___
law ___	engineering ___	history ___	psychology ___

Collocations related to education

2 Match adjectives 1–7 to the nouns a–g to make education collocations. More than one answer is possible for some of the collocations.

Adjectives
1 rote
2 critical
3 higher
4 academic
5 continuous
6 formal
7 educational

Nouns
a standards
b education
c dishonesty
d assessment
e learning
f thinking
g examinations

3 Complete sentences 1–6 with an education collocation from Exercise 2 on page 24.

1 If you need to memorise lots of information, _____ is a good method to use.
2 If you need to evaluate information, you need _____ skills.
3 In many countries, students sit _____ in order to graduate.
4 Access to _____ is often determined by performance in university entrance examinations.
5 In some countries, progress is measured by _____ instead of by end-of-term examinations.
6 Some people worry that without examinations, _____ will decline.

Expressing quantity

4 Expressions 1–6 are useful for describing quantity. Match them with the percentages a–f.

1 nearly half __   a 85%
2 the vast majority __   b 75%
3 a small minority __   c 46%
4 three quarters __   d 31%
5 just under a third __ e 24%
6 roughly one in four __ f 15%

> **Exam tip**
>
> To describe data more effectively and show that you have a wide vocabulary, learn how to express proportion in different ways.

5 The bar chart below shows the results of a survey of how people felt about examinations. Complete sentences 1–6 below, which describe the chart, using expressions 1–6 from Exercise 4.

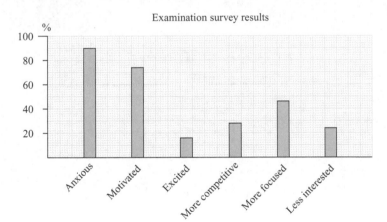

Examination survey results

> **Watch out**
>
> Use the definite article *the* with *majority*, e.g. *The majority of students liked physics.*
> Use the indefinite article *a* with *minority*, e.g. *A minority of students chose art.*

1 _____ of those surveyed said they found the challenge exciting.
2 _____ of respondents said they felt anxious.
3 _____ said they felt more competitive.
4 _____ of those surveyed replied that they felt more focused.
5 _____ indicated that examinations made them lose interest in their studies.
6 _____ of those who responded said they felt motivated to work harder.

Part 2: Exam skills

Task 1: Comparing and contrasting information

 Exam information: Making comparisons

For Task 1, you may be asked to write about information presented in one or more bar charts or pie charts. For this type of data, you are expected not just to describe, but also to compare the information.

1 Read rules 1–6 for making comparisons in the table. Then complete the table with examples a–f.

Rules	Example sentences
Use comparative forms to compare two or more items:	
1 *more / fewer / less* + noun… + *than*	
2 adjectives of one syllable + *-er* + noun… + *than*	
3 *more / less* + adjective of two or more syllables	
Use superlative forms to compare one item with the remainder of a group:	
4 adjectives of one syllable + *-est*	
5 *the most / least* + adjective of two or more syllables	
To express similarity, use:	
6 *as* + adjective + *as*	

a   Science-related subjects were more popular than arts-related subjects.
b   More students sat examinations in science subjects than in arts subjects.
c   Business studies was nearly as popular as chemistry.
d   The highest percentage of students gaining top marks was in mathematics.
e   A higher percentage of students gained top marks in mathematics than in chemistry.
f   The most popular subject was mathematics.

Mathematics 45%
Biology 30%
Chemistry 34%
Business studies 32%
Media studies 13%
History 16%
Philosophy 14%
Sociology 16%

☐ Number of entries
▨ Percentage awarded A or A*

20   40   60   80   thousands

2 Complete sentences 1–6 with a comparative or superlative form.

1   Nearly _____ many students sat the business studies exam _____ did the chemistry exam.
2   The percentage of students gaining top marks in business studies was slightly _____ than the percentage of students achieving top marks in chemistry.
3   The _____ popular subjects were history, philosophy, and sociology.
4   The philosophy examination was taken by _____ students than the history examination.
5   However, a _____ percentage of students taking the philosophy exam gained top marks.
6   The _____ percentage of students gaining top marks was in media studies.

Exam tip

Use adverbs to make your comparisons more exact.

1 To emphasise a difference, use: *many, much, far,* and *significantly,* e.g. **Many** more students sat examinations in science subjects.

2 For small differences, use: *slightly* or *nearly as ... as,* e.g. *The number of passes was **slightly** higher than the number of fails. Males did **nearly as** well as females.*

Describing information in bar charts

Exam tip

You can use expressions such as *in contrast* to express difference, or *the same* to express similarity.

3 Read sentences 1–4 below. Write S if the sentence expresses similarity and D if it expresses difference. Underline the words which helped you decide.

1 The percentage of top marks was quite high in subjects such as mathematics, which are traditionally regarded as difficult. On the other hand, the percentage of top marks was relatively low in subjects such as media studies, which are commonly regarded as 'soft'. _____

2 Whereas 45% of mathematics candidates gained top marks, only 13% of media studies candidates gained top marks. _____

3 Similar numbers of students sat examinations in business studies and in chemistry. _____

4 Sixteen percent of students gained top marks in both history and sociology. _____

4 Rewrite sentences 1–5 using the words in brackets.

1 More female candidates than male candidates passed their English examinations. (fewer)

_____

2 The same number of males and females achieved a passing grade in mathematics. (as... as)

_____

3 Men did well in technology-related subjects; women, in contrast, did well in language-related subjects. (whereas)

_____

4 The number of passes in psychology was higher for female candidates than for male candidates. (lower)

_____

5 Nearly as many female students as male students passed the economics exam. (similar)

_____

Watch out

Use *fewer / fewest* with countable nouns, e.g. *Fewer student took physics.*
Use *less / least* with uncountable nouns, e.g. *There was less interest in physics.*

Task 2: Selecting and organising ideas

5 Read the Task 2 question below and compare the notes below and the essay plan that follows. Then answer questions 1–4.

1 What is the writer's position on examinations?
2 Which of her ideas has the writer omitted from body paragraphs one and two?
3 Why do you think the writer has omitted these points?
4 Why has the writer chosen to list her main ideas in this order?

> **Exam tip**
>
> Once you have taken a position on the question and generated ideas, you should decide which of your ideas to include and in what order. If you have a plan before you start writing, this will help you to focus and write more quickly.

Success in formal 'pen and paper' examinations is often seen to be a sign of intelligence. To what extent do you agree with the view that formal examinations measure intelligence?

Notes

What are the ideas?	Evidence for?	Evidence against?
Idea in the question: Exams measure intelligence	Exams can be designed to include a variety of tasks to measure different kinds of intelligence People who do well in exams often do well in other types of tasks, e.g. assignments	Pen and paper exams are often predictable – students can prepare by rote learning There are many ways of cheating in exams People often perform poorly in examinations because they are anxious, not because they lack intelligence
Alternative idea: There are different types of intelligence, which can only be measured in different ways	Some people are better at expressing intelligence in different ways, e.g. by speaking or carrying out a task Many people who did poorly in exams are successful in fields that require intelligence, e.g. technology or business.	Other methods of measuring intelligence could be less objective and systematic There is probably no definitive proof of whether there is one kind of intelligence or several kinds of intelligence

Essay plan

Introduction:	Measuring intelligence is a difficult task
Body paragraph 1:	Idea in the question: Exams measure intelligence
	Evidence for: people who do well in exams often do well in other types of tasks, e.g. assignments
	Evidence against: pen & paper exams are often predictable – students can prepare by rote learning; there are many ways of cheating in exams; people often perform poorly in examinations because they are anxious, not because they lack intelligence
Body paragraph 2:	Other possible idea: there are probably different types of intelligence, which can only be measured in different ways

	Evidence against: there is probably no definitive proof of whether there is one kind of intelligence or several kinds of intelligence
	Evidence for: Some people are better at expressing intelligence in different ways, e.g. by speaking or carrying out a task; many people who did poorly in exams, are successful in fields that require intelligence, e.g. technology, business
Conclusion:	'pen and paper' exams probably useful for measuring certain kinds of intelligence, but have limitations; other methods are needed

Writing an essay outline

6 Read the Task 2 question below and identify the problem presented. Complete the table with at least one positive consequence and drawback for each point.

Education systems do not always provide learners with enough training to do well in exams. Some students attend private 'cram schools' for extra coaching in test-taking techniques. What is your view of this practice?

Exam tip

Explaining the advantages and disadvantages of different ideas means you can demonstrate more advanced language skills.

Notes

What are the possible solutions?	Positive consequences?	Drawbacks?
Solution in the question: Cram schools	Cram schools do a good job - many students who attend such schools do well in exams	Cram schools teach students to be 'test wise' rather than to learn
Alternative solution: We should ensure schools are good enough for all students	In countries with exams that properly reflect the curriculum, there are few cram schools	Cram schools will always exist because it is human nature to want to gain an advantage

7 Write an essay plan defending the alternative solution in Exercise 6 and including the most appropriate points.

	Essay plan
	Introduction:
	Body paragraph 1:
	Body paragraph 2:
	Conclusion:

Exam practice

WRITING TASK 1: Describe a bar chart

You should spend about 20 minutes on this task.

> The graph compares the percentage of international and the percentage of UK students gaining second class degrees or better at a major UK university.
>
> Summarise the information by selecting and reporting the main features.

Write at least 150 words.

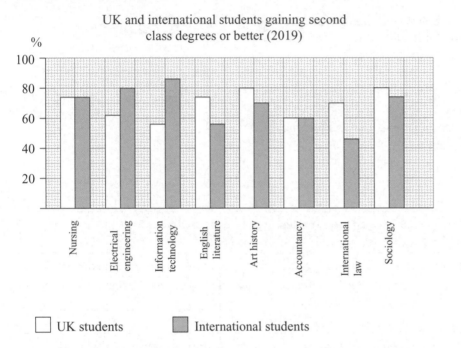

UK and international students gaining second class degrees or better (2019)

WRITING TASK 2: Write an essay evaluating an idea

You should spend about 40 minutes on this task.

Write about the following topic:

> Many people believe that formal 'pen and paper' examinations are not the best method of assessing educational achievement.
>
> What is your view of examinations?

Give reasons for your answer and include any relevant examples from your own knowledge or experience.

Write at least 250 words.

Exam tutor

1 If you are presented with a bar chart in Task 1, should you focus mainly on describing the information in detail?

2 When should you use comparative forms and when should you use superlative forms?

3 When referring to percentages or numbers should you always use the exact numbers presented in the visual prompt?

4 What is the benefit of having a plan before you start writing your Task 2 essay?

5 What is the benefit of discussing the advantages and disadvantages of different ideas in your essay?

4 Biodiversity

Language development | Nature and environment expressions; Expressions to describe cause and effect
Exam skills | Task 1: Describing a process; Combining sentences in a process description; Task 2: Writing in an academic style
Exam practice | Task 1: Describe a process; Task 2: Write an essay proposing solutions

Part 1: Language development

Nature and environment expressions

1 Match the pictures 1–6 with the natural habitats a–f.

a estuary   c wetlands   e grasslands
b forest   d desert   f rainforest

2 The expressions in the box describe sources of damage to the environment. Complete sentences 1–7 using these expressions.

oil spills	intensive farming	strip mining	logging
acid rain	overgrazing	global warming	

1 _____ in wheat-growing countries like Canada has led to the loss of natural grasslands.
2 _____ causes damage to forests as well as limestone monuments.
3 Indiscriminate _____ of tropical hardwoods has contributed to the destruction of rainforests.
4 _____ of grasslands by cattle and sheep is associated with soil erosion and desertification.
5 Off-shore _____ frequently result in damage to wetlands and the many species that live there.
6 The thinning of the arctic icecap has been attributed to _____.
7 _____ for minerals near river banks is linked to soil erosion and degradation of estuaries.

Expressions to describe cause and effect

3 Underline the verbs that express cause and effect in Exercise 2 on page 32. Then answer questions 1–3 below.

   1 Which verbs express a definite cause-and-effect relationship?
   2 Which verbs suggest a cause-and-effect relationship?
   3 How is *contribute to* different from *cause*?

 **Watch out**

If you do not have clear evidence, use an expression such as *is/are associated with*.

4 Structures that can be used to express cause-and-effect relationships are listed in the table. Complete the table with example sentences a–e for each structure 1–5.

Grammatical structure	Example
1 *because* + dependent clause	
2 *because of* / *due to* + noun phrase	
3 *therefore* / *consequently* / *as a result* + clause	
4 *so* + clause	
5 *so* + adjective or adverb + *that* + clause	

  a Wetlands have been damaged, so many unique species are now endangered.
  b Many unique species are now endangered because wetlands have been damaged.
  c Many unique species are now endangered because of damage to wetlands.
  d Wetlands have been so damaged that many unique species are now endangered.
  e Wetlands have been damaged; as a result, many unique species are now endangered.

5 Rewrite sentences 1–4 below using the words in brackets. Make any other changes necessary.

   1 Land has been farmed so intensively that there has been a significant decline in biodiversity. (contributed to)
      Intensive farming _____.
   2 Loss of vegetation has caused a decline in the insect population. (consequently)
      Vegetation _____.
   3 Because there are fewer insects, the small animals that feed on them have moved elsewhere. (so)
      There are _____.
   4 The disappearance of prey species has resulted in fewer predators such as owls. (because of)
      There has been _____.

! **Watch out**

Conjunctive adverbs and the expressions *therefore, consequently, as a result* should be punctuated with a full stop or semicolon before them and a comma after them, e.g. *Wetlands have been damaged;* **as a result**, *many unique species are now endangered.*

Part 2: Exam skills

Task 1: Describing a process

1 Read the two process descriptions below. Use information from the second description to complete the flowchart.

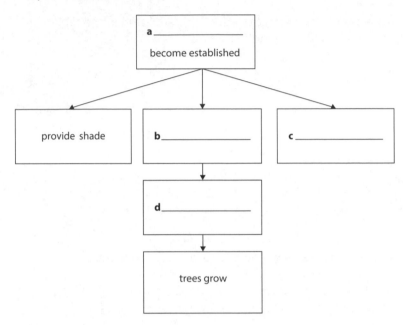

> **Exam tip**
> Task 1 visual prompts sometimes take the form of diagrams or maps which illustrate a process of change.

1 Clear cutting

The flow chart illustrates the process of clear cutting, a logging practice which involves the complete removal of trees from a given area.

Firstly, access roads to the area are cut. Secondly, the entire crop of standing trees is felled by mechanized harvesters. The trees are then extracted, and brought to the roadside.

Once the trees have been extracted, they are processed by chain saw. The limbs and tree tops are removed. The stems are 'bucked', that is, cut into logs of a specified length. The logs are then sorted by size and loaded onto logging trucks for transport to the sawmill.

In the final stage of clear cutting, the land is prepared for future harvests. The remaining scrub is gathered into large piles and burnt.

2 Forest re-growth

Following a period of widespread deforestation, forest regrowth occurs over a series of phases.

The first plants to grow are 'pioneer' plants, which can survive in harsh conditions. They provide shade, gather moisture, and return organic material to the soil. In doing so, they create the conditions for other plants to thrive.

In the second phase of regrowth, shrubs emerge. They quickly cover the ground, crowding out the pioneers. However, they too eventually die off as young trees push through the brush. Within ten years, trees finally take over, preventing light from reaching the forest floor.

2 Underline the verbs in the process descriptions on page 34. Then decide whether you would normally use the active or the passive voice when:

   a the process is natural.

   b there is a human agent.

💡 Exam tip

To make a process description more readable, include several stages of a process in one sentence. Combine sentences with the same subject by removing the repeated subjects and linking with commas and *and* for the final clause, e.g.
Wetlands reduce flooding. Wetlands protect the shoreline from waves. Wetlands improve water quality.
Wetlands reduce flooding, ~~. Wetlands~~ protect the shoreline from waves, and ~~. Wetlands~~ improve water quality.

Combining sentences in a process description

3 Notice the different techniques used to combine the groups of sentences 1–6 below. Join each group of sentences without looking at the model texts.

   1 The first plants to grow are pioneer plants. Pioneer plants can survive in harsh conditions.

   _____

   2 Pioneer plants provide shade. Pioneer plants gather moisture. Pioneer plants return organic material to the soil.

   _____

   3 Shrubs quickly cover the ground. Shrubs crowd out the pioneers.

   _____

   4 However, shrubs too eventually die off. Young trees push through the brush.

   _____

   5 The logs are sorted by size. The logs are loaded onto logging trucks. They are transported to the sawmill.

   _____

   6 The trees have been extracted. The trees are processed by chain saw.

   _____

4 Study the two maps about changes in land use on Borneo below. Then rewrite the passage, using the passive voice and combining sentences where appropriate.

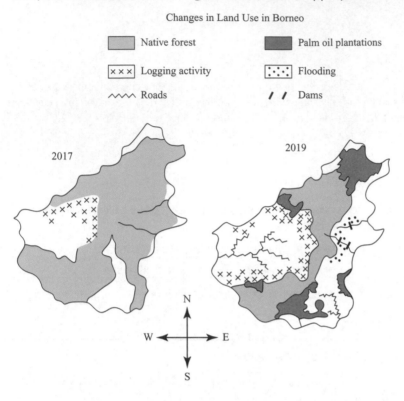

Changes in Land Use in Borneo

Native forest		Palm oil plantations	
x x x Logging activity		Flooding	
Roads		Dams	

2017

2019

N
W ← → E
S

Exam tip
The passive voice is often used when the subject of the action is unknown or less important than the action itself, e.g. *People associate overgrazing with desertification – Overgrazing is associated with desertification.*

The maps show changes that have taken place on the island between 1970 and 2019.

Over the fifty-year period, people removed large areas of native forest in the north-east and south. They partially replaced native forest in the north-east and south with palm oil plantations. The area of intact forest in the west shrank. People built roads. Logging also increased. Workers built dams in the east. The dams flooded the area. The dams further reduced the extent of native forest.

Exam tip
Use signposting language in your description to mark the stages of the process.
Examples: **Firstly**, *access roads to the area are cut.* **In the final stage** *of clear cutting, the land is prepared for future harvests.* One signpost4 at the start, one or two in the middle and one at the end are usually sufficient.

Your rewrite of the passage:

Task 2: Writing in an academic style

5 Compare the introductions and first body paragraphs of two responses to the question below. Underline the differences and answer questions 1–2.

1 What is the main difference between these two responses?
2 What are the main characteristics of the style of the second response?

Many species of plants and animals have come and gone throughout the history of the Earth. From this perspective, extinction can be seen as part of a natural process. Some people have argued that we should not, therefore, make heroic efforts to preserve the natural habitats of endangered plants and animals when doing so would conflict with human interests.

To what extent do you agree with this view?

Response 1

In my opinion, it's true that humans and animals sometimes have conflicting interests. Everybody exploits animals for food and clothing, and farmers have used more and more wild land for farming. But should we keep on doing this?

In parts of the world where the population is growing, and there isn't enough food to go around, the conflict between humans and animals is really awful. For example, if you go to Africa, you can see large nature reserves next to really poor human settlements. I love the idea of elephants and lions living in the wild. But it's often the poor farmer living nearby who loses out.

Response 2

It may be true that humans and animals sometimes have conflicting interests. Most people exploit animals for food and clothing, and farmers have brought ever increasing areas of wild land into cultivation. However, whether this process should continue is a question that needs careful consideration.

In parts of the world where the population is growing and resources are scarce, the conflict between humans and animals is particularly problematic. This can be seen in parts of Africa, for example, where large nature reserves lie next to very poor human settlements. People living thousands of miles away may value the idea of elephants and lions living in the wild. However, it is often the poor farmer living nearby who is denied access to land and potential earnings.

6 The table below outlines four characteristics of academic style. Complete the table with examples from the texts in Exercise 5 on page 37.

Characteristics of academic style	Examples from responses 1 and 2	
	Informal style	Academic style
Academic style tends to be less personal. Avoid: • overusing personal pronouns and adjectives (e.g. *I, you, my, your*) • addressing the reader directly	*In my opinion, it's true*	*It may be true*
Academic style tends to be less emotional. Avoid: • exaggeration (e.g. *totally, perfect*), • emotive words (e.g. *terrible, adore*) • words that express value judgments (e.g. *immoral*).	*Everybody exploits*	*Most people exploit*
Academic style normally requires: • fewer conjunctions (e.g. *and, but*) • more subordinators (e.g. *whereas, because*) • more sentence linkers (e.g. *nevertheless, therefore*).	*but*	*However,*
Academic style is more formal. Avoid: • contracted forms (e.g. *isn't, he's*) • the words *get, a lot of* and *really* • double comparatives (e.g. *more and more*) • phrasal verbs (e.g. *take up, break out*), • colloquial expressions or sayings (e.g. *every coin has two sides*)	*it's*	*it is*

7 Rewrite the second half of the essay below in a more academic style.

But if you think about plants, there are more pros to conservation. Wild plants aren't just beautiful. They can also be really valuable. Throughout history, people have used wild plants to make medicines, like aspirin for example. And if some standard crops get diseases, you could use wild plants to develop new kinds of crops. There are a lot of plants that we haven't even discovered yet, so we don't know what they might be useful for.

In my opinion, it's worth trying to protect nature because wild animals and plants are really special and they could be life savers. But we have to remember that people are important too. So, we have to do it in a fair way.

 **Watch out**

If writing in an academic style is new to you, make sure your style and message are clear.

8 Rewrite sentences 1–2 below to make them clearer and easier to read. Remove unnecessary words and divide long sentences, if required.

1 It could be argued, though the opposite view might be equally true, that the tendency that many people have to acquire riches and material wealth is one of several possible factors that may encourage people to exploit the natural environment excessively.

2 It is possible that some people may believe that environmental degradation is a process that cannot be avoided in the long term because the countries of the world do not have a way or means of enforcing environmental agreements which their leaders may have committed themselves to, possibly for the wrong reasons, for instance simply to create a favourable impression in the mass media and television.

Part 3: Exam practice

WRITING TASK 1: Describe a process

You should spend about 20 minutes on this task. Write at least 150 words.

The flow chart illustrates the consequences of deforestation.
Summarise the information by selecting and reporting the main features.

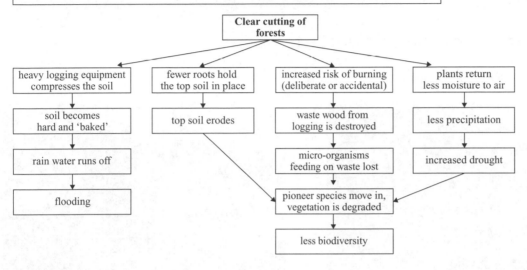

WRITING TASK 2: Write an essay proposing solutions

You should spend about 40 minutes on this task. Write about the following topic:

The importance of biodiversity is being more widely recognised as increasing numbers of species come under threat. What can be done to maintain biodiversity?

Give reasons for your answer and include any relevant examples from your own knowledge or experience. Write at least 250 words.

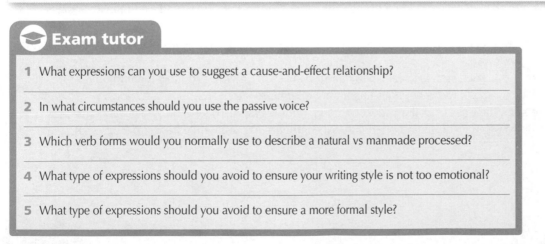

🎓 Exam tutor

1 What expressions can you use to suggest a cause-and-effect relationship?

2 In what circumstances should you use the passive voice?

3 Which verb forms would you normally use to describe a natural vs manmade processed?

4 What type of expressions should you avoid to ensure your writing style is not too emotional?

5 What type of expressions should you avoid to ensure a more formal style?

5 Global English

Part 1: Language development

Expressions associated with languages

1 The expressions in the box are all related to language. Use each expression once (in the singular or plural form) to complete sentences 1–8.

bilingual	second language	lingua franca	minority language
mother tongue	non-native	official language	standard form

1 The majority of people living in the US, the UK, Canada, Australia, and New Zealand speak English as their _____.
2 English is a(n) _____ in a further fifty-three countries, including India and the Philippines.
3 English is the most widely taught _____ in the world.
4 English is often regarded as a _____ because it is used by so many people around the world for so many purposes.
5 The ratio of _____ speakers to native speakers of English is roughly three to one.
6 People who can speak two languages fluently are referred to as _____.
7 There are many varieties of English spoken throughout the world; There is no single _____.
8 Some people fear that the spread of English will contribute to the disappearance of _____.

Reporting verbs for different functions

2 Reporting verbs for different functions are presented in the table below. Add the verbs in the box to the most appropriate category 1–4.

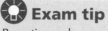 **Exam tip**

Contrasting your opinion with other points of view allows you to present a stronger argument.

| bilingual | second language | lingua franca | minority language |
| mother tongue | non-native | official language | standard form |

Purpose	Examples
1 to state a position or belief	*believe, suspect, say, argue, insist*
2 to show agreement	*agree, accept, acknowledge, support*
3 to show disagreement	*disagree, doubt, question, dismiss, refute*
4 to make a suggestion or recommendation	*suggest, recommend, advocate*

Emphatic, neutral and tentative reporting

3 Underline the more tentative reporting verb in italics in sentences 1–7.

1 Many people *insist / argue* that there is one 'best' variety of English.
2 However, I *question / refute* the idea that one variety of the language is better than another.
3 Some people *doubt / deny* the value of a bilingual education.
4 Others *accept / advocate* the idea of a bilingual education, even for very young children.
5 I would *urge / suggest* educational authorities do all they can to promote minority languages.
6 Linguists *suspect / maintain* that within a century, there will only be a few languages spoken.
7 Other people *dismiss / doubt* the idea that all but two or three languages will die out.

Exam tip

Reporting verbs can be tentative (e.g. *suspect*), neutral (e.g. *agree*), or emphatic (e.g. *assert*). If you have strong evidence to support a point, use a more emphatic verb. If not, use a neutral or tentative verb.

4 Different reporting verbs are followed by different structures. Match the structures 1–4 with examples a–d.

1 reporting verb + *whether* + clause

2 reporting verb + noun or noun phrase

3 reporting verb + gerund (*-ing*)

4 reporting verb + object + infinitive

a Most people would support the idea of providing free tuition.

b I would urge the government to provide free tuition.

c Many people question whether governments should provide free tuition.

d Educators recommend providing free tuition.

Exam tip

Reporting verbs can often be followed by more than one type of structure, e.g.
reporting verb + *whether* + clause: *Others question whether schools should promote …*
reporting verb + noun phrase: *Others question the feasibility of promoting …*

Part 2: Exam skills

Task 1: Creating a coherent structure

1 Look at the diagram below and put the paragraphs a–d that describe it in the correct order.

⬡ Exam tip

There is no one 'correct' way to structure a Task 1 description. However, your Task 1 response is more likely to be judged coherent and cohesive if it follows a common pattern.

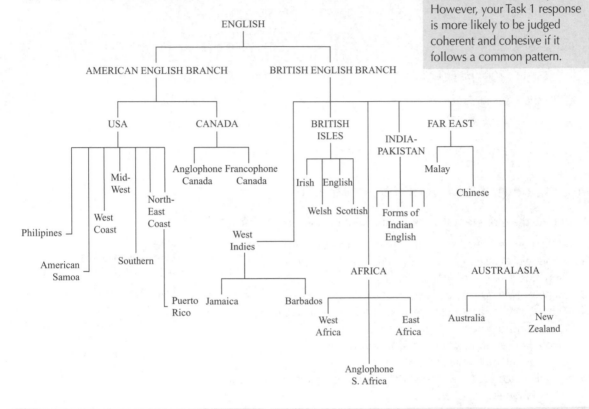

a The American branch is largely restricted to the American continent. It comprises the varieties of English spoken in the different regions of the United States itself, as well as in Canada. Beyond the continent, the extent of its influence is limited to the Philippines in the Far East and American Samoa in the Pacific.

b In brief, the diagram shows that the reach of English has extended to virtually every region of the world, and, in doing so, has developed numerous varieties.

c The diagram shows the varieties of English spoken throughout the world and how they are related.

d There are two main types of English: British English and American English. The British English Branch is geographically widespread. It extends across several continents from the West Indies, through the British Isles themselves, Africa, the Indian subcontinent, the Far East and Australasia. In addition to the four varieties of English spoken in the British Isles (i.e. in Ireland, Wales, Scotland and England), it includes a large number of other varieties, for instance Jamaican English, South African English, and Australian English.

2 Read paragraphs a–d in Exercise 1 on page 42 again and answer questions 1–3.

   1 Which paragraphs refer to the whole diagram and which paragraphs refer to parts of the diagram?

   2 How is the introductory paragraph different from the concluding paragraph.?

   3 Do the body paragraphs give general information first and then specific information, or vice versa?

3 Look at the Task 1 instructions below. Then read sentences a–d and answer questions 1–4.

> The diagram illustrates the percentage of the world population that speaks minority, mid-sized, and dominant languages. Summarise the information by selecting and reporting the main features.

a

The diagram shows the percentage of the world population that speaks minority, mid-sized, and dominant languages.

b

The diagram shows the number of languages classified as minority, mid-sized, or dominant, and the proportion of people in the world that speak them.

c

The diagram shows that although many languages are spoken throughout the world, the size of their respective speech communities varies enormously.

d

The diagram shows that a very small number of languages (approximately 100) hold a dominant position, whereas more than half of the world's languages are spoken by a very small percentage of the world population (0.2%).

   1 Which of the sentences a–d works well as an introduction?

   2 Which sentence works well as a conclusion?

   3 What is the problem with sentence a?

   4 Why might you not want to use sentence d as an introduction or conclusion?

Introductions and conclusions

4 Complete the sentences for introduction and the conclusion for the bar chart below.

! Watch out

Do not copy the exact words of the task instructions. Rephrasing the instructions in your own words shows more language skill.

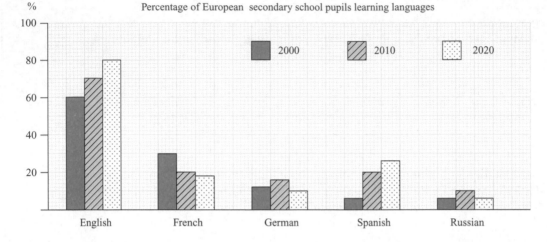

Percentage of European secondary school pupils learning languages

1 **Introduction:**

The bar chart shows ...

_____

_____

_____

2 **Main paragraph:**

In terms of rank order, English was by far the most commonly studied second language, followed by French, Spanish, German and Russian. English also experienced the most significant growth over the two decades, rising from 60 percent of secondary school learners to 80 percent. Spanish also gained in popularity, most notably between 2000 and 2010, when the percentage of those studying Spanish nearly trebled. German and Russian both experienced and increase between 2000 and 2010 and a fall over the following ten years. The study of French, on the other hand, fell over the 20-year period, steeply at first, and then more gradually to just under 20 percent of learners.

3 **Conclusion:**

In summary, ...

_____

_____

_____

Task 2: Developing an introduction

> 💡 **Exam tip**
>
> It is important to make a good first impression by writing a strong opening
> paragraph. Introductions often contain elements that make it easier for the
> reader to follow the rest of the essay.

5 Read the Task 2 question below and the introduction that follows. Match each section of the
introduction to one of the functions a–g.

a   state the topic of the essay: *This essay is about ...*
b   write something about the general context: *In recent years ...*
c   explain why the topic is interesting, relevant or important: *X is interesting/relevant/important because*
d   present a viewpoint that they go on to challenge: *Some people believe that ...*
e   present their own viewpoint: *In my view, ...*
f   state the purpose of the essay: *The aim of this essay is to ...*
g   outline the structure of the essay: *This essay will firstly ..., secondly ..., thirdly ...*

As the English language becomes more widespread, some speakers of other languages fear that
English loanwords are gradually replacing perfectly adequate native words.
To what extent do you believe that people should seek to protect the 'purity' of their language from
the influence of English?

There is no doubt that English is becoming increasingly ——————— | 1 _____ |
important as a language of international communication in
the fields of science, trade, entertainment, and international
relations. Not surprisingly, English words have appeared in ——————— | 2 _____ |
many other languages throughout the world from Japanese to
French. This has prompted some people to seek to defend their ——————— | 3 _____ |
languages from this type of change. I would argue however, that
these efforts are likely to prove futile. ——————— | 4 _____ |

6 Answer questions 1–2 about the introduction in Exercise 5

1   How would you describe the overall organisation of the introductory paragraph? Does it begin with the
writer's opinion and then explain the context, or vice versa?
2   Why has the writer presented his / her own view last?

Presenting your view effectively

7 Read the Task 2 question below and sentences 1–5. For each sentence, indicate its function a–g, as listed in Exercise 5 on page 45.

> With regard to second language learning, the effectiveness of out-of-class learning is well-established. What are the best ways of learning a second language outside of a classroom situation?

1 I believe the success of out-of-class learning suggests that not all language learning needs to be classroom based.
2 However, in many cases, additional languages are learned not in the classroom, but through exposure to a language in day-to-day activities.
3 Around the world, people who speak only their mother tongue are probably outnumbered by those who speak one or more additional languages.
4 In this essay I will outline what I consider to be the three most effective ways of independent language learning.
5 Many people assume that the classroom is the best place to learn a second language.

8 Arrange sentences 1–5 from Exercise 7 in the most logical order.

9 Complete the introduction to an essay about teaching second languages using the expressions in the box.

right approach	the most effective methods	therefore
the world becomes	increasingly important	I will outline

> As (1) _____ more integrated, the ability to speak a second language is becoming (2) _____, not just for individuals, but also for nations. The teaching of second or other languages is labour-intensive and (3) _____ costly, so it is important that the (4) _____ is taken. In this essay, (5) _____ what I consider to be (6) _____ of language teaching in a classroom context.

10 Write an introduction for the Task 2 question below.

> Sometimes misunderstandings occur among people from different cultures, even those who can communicate in a common language. What factors can contribute to the breakdown of cross-cultural communication?

🔅 Exam tip

Use more emphatic verbs to challenge viewpoints, e.g. *Some people insist…* . Use more neutral verbs to express your own position, e.g. *I would suggest…*

Part 3: Exam practice

WRITING TASK 1: Describe a diagram

You should spend about 20 minutes on this task. Write at least 150 words.

The diagram shows the relationship among a number of different languages. Summarise the information by selecting and reporting the main features.

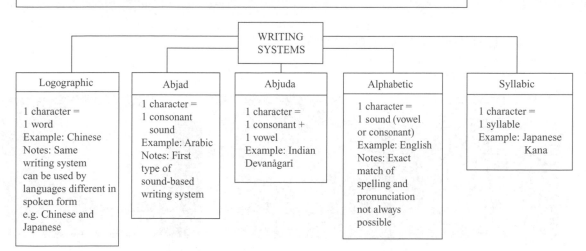

WRITING TASK 2: Write an essay evaluating a solution

You should spend about 40 minutes on this task. Write about the following topic:

As languages such as English, Spanish and Mandarin become more widely spoken, there is a concern that many minority languages may disappear. Some countries have taken steps to protect minority languages. What is your view of this practice?

Give reasons for your answer and include any relevant examples from your own knowledge or experience. Write at least 250 words.

🎓 Exam tutor

1 Which reporting verbs can you use to express agreement and which to express disagreement?

2 In your Task 1 introduction, should you repeat the wording in the exam instructions or mainly use your own words?

3 What elements could you include in a Task 2 introductions?

4 In a Task 2 introduction, should you express your opinion at the beginning or at the end?
Would you normally use a more emphatic or more tentative reporting verb to express your point of view.

6 The Internet

Language development | Technology expressions; Adjectives for highlighting key points;
Language for moderating statements
Exam skills | Task 1: Interpreting information in tables; Writing general statements and
supporting details; Task 2: Planning an essay; Developing a paragraph
Exam practice | Task 1: Describe a table; Task 2: Write an essay evaluating an idea

Part 1: Language development

Technology expressions

1 Match the photos 1–6 to the expressions a–f in the box.

a streaming music	b social networking	c online banking
d browsing the news	e online shopping	f sending and receiving emails

Adjectives for highlighting key points

2 Match the adjectives a–f with the correct definitions 1–6.

a distinctive   1 affecting many people or places
b main   2 easy to see
c noticeable   3 important
d significant   4 most important
e underlying   5 basic but not obvious
f widespread   6 easily recognized because special

> **Exam tip**
> In Writing Task 1, it is important
> to highlight key points. Different
> adjectives, e.g. *main* and
> *significant*, indicate how a point
> is important.

3 Complete sentences 1–5 with the most appropriate adjective from Exercise 2 on page 48. Notice how they form collocations with the nouns in italics.

1 At first glance, the most _____ *change* was in the growing popularity of social networking.
2 The graph shows that the spread of wireless technology has a _____ *pattern*.
3 While there was some variation in the use of online auction sites, the _____ *trend* has been upward.
4 Although price is undoubtedly a factor, the _____ *reason* customers chose the newer devices is because of their wide range of features.
5 The _____ *distribution* of towns in that region made investment in infrastructure worthwhile.

Language for moderating statements

4 Add the words in the box to the table below.

| tend | many | rarely | might | probably | most |
| | often | appear | may | could | |

Type of modifier	Examples
Quantifiers	*some* _____
Verbs	*seem* _____
Modal verbs	*can* _____
Adverbs of frequency	*sometimes* _____
Adverbs of probability	*possibly* _____

5 Use words from Exercise 4 to modify statements 1–5. Make any other changes necessary for an appropriate academic style.

1 People over the age of 60 cannot grasp new technology.
   Some people over the age of 60…
2 Excessive use of social media causes mental health problems.
3 Online shopping is addictive.
4 Too much screen time makes children lazy.
5 The world's problems will be solved by advances in science and technology.

❗ Watch out

Too many modifiers can make the meaning of your sentences unclear, e.g. *It is possible that in some circumstances excessive use of social media can cause some people to become anxious.*

💡 Exam tip

Task 1 statements can be straightforward because the prompt provides information to support your claims, e.g. *The graph shows that the spread of wireless technology has a distinctive regional pattern.*
For Task 2 you do not have supporting evidence, so statements should be more moderate, e.g. *The rapid spread of new technologies **can sometimes** be socially disruptive.*

Part 2: Exam skills

Task 1: Interpreting information in tables

1 Study the table below which shows the percentage of time Internet users spent on the six most popular online activities in 2008 and 2018. Then read and compare the two responses and answer questions 1–3.

1 Which response is more satisfactory? Why?
2 Which sentences contain the main points?
3 In each response, where is the detailed information in relation to the general statements?

Activity	Share of time 2018	Share of time 2008
Social networking	22	14
Searching for information	21	15
Email/messaging	19	27
Reading content	18	27
Streaming music and video	15	13
Shopping	5	4

Response 1

The table shows that there were significant changes in how people spent their time online over the ten-year period.

The percentage of time spent on social networking sites increased sharply from fourteen percent to twenty-two percent This was similar to the change in time spent on searching for information. Communicating online through email and messaging, on the other hand decreased from twenty-seven to nineteen percent. This was also true of reading online content, which fell from twenty-seven to eighteen percent There were small rises in the remaining two categories: streaming music and video and online shopping. These increased from thirteen to fifteen percent and from four to five percent respectively.

Overall, the way that users spent their time on the Internet varied significantly, with some activities, such as social networking, becoming more popular and others becoming less popular.

Response 2

The table shows that there were significant changes in how people spent their time online over the ten-year period.

One of the most significant changes was in the way users communicated online. The use of social media increased significantly from fourteen to twenty-two percent. However, this appears to have been at the expense of other forms of online communication, namely email and instant messaging, which fell from twenty-seven to nineteen percent of all online activity. Another noticeable trend was the change in time spent finding and reading content online. In 2018, people spent a higher percentage of time searching for information (twenty-one percent versus fifteen percent), but a smaller proportion of time reading it (eighteen percent as opposed to twenty-seven percent in 2008). There were only relatively small changes in the remaining two categories: streaming music and video and online shopping. These increased from thirteen to fifteen percent and from four to five percent respectively.

Overall, in 2018, people continued to spend the largest proportion of their time engaging with other people and information online; however, their ways of doing so had changed.

2 Study the table below and answer questions 1–4.

1 Focus on the bottom row. What general points can you make from the data shown?

2 Now focus on the regions listed in the first column. How could you group them into categories? Consider levels of technological development.

3 Change your focus to the percentages listed in the third column. Which regions have the largest percentages of internet users? Which have the smallest? How could this information relate to how you have grouped the regions?

4 Look at the data in the last column. What connections can you make with information in the other columns?

World regions	Number of Internet users (millions)	Internet users as % of population	Growth in Internet use 2008–2018
Asia	2,195	50%	1,820%
Europe	720	88%	585%
Africa	495	36%	10,820%
Latin America	445	67%	2,360%
North America	325	89%	200%
Middle East	175	67%	5,185%
Australia/Oceania	30	80%	275%
TOTAL	4,385	57%	1,115%

Writing general statements and supporting details

3 Write three general statements about the information in the table above. Then develop each of your general statements with one or two supporting details.

The table shows that over the ten-year period there was an exponential increase in Internet use worldwide. The number of Internet users expanded more than tenfold, with the proportion of the world's population online reaching fifty-seven percent in 2020.

Task 2: Planning an essay

Task 2 essays can be organised in different ways. Some patterns of organisation can allow you to show more skills in language and argumentation than others.

4   Study the Task 2 question and the essay plan below. What are the strengths and weaknesses of this plan?

> To what extent does the Internet increase loneliness and social isolation?

Essay outline

Introduction:	The Internet is important in modern life, but it can also be a double-edged sword
Body paragraph 1:	Idea in the question: Internet can increase social isolation
Evidence for negative effect:	**a** young people who spend a lot of time online cannot develop social skills or make real friends
	b online activities like gaming can be so addictive, people can disconnect from their families; e.g. parents neglecting children
	c Evidence for: people at work spend so much time reading emails, no time to speak to colleagues, can be bad for teamwork
Body paragraph 2:	Other possible idea: Internet can bring people closer together
Evidence for positive effect:	**d** people who cannot go out easily because of injury or disability can keep in touch with friends online
	e when members of a family live far apart, the Internet is cheaper for communicating than phone calls
	f through social networking, friends can meet friends of friends
	g Email can be more useful than the phone for working together because there is a written record of the communication
Conclusion:	The Internet can bring people together if used in the right way

5 Look at the alternative essay plan below. Indicate where you would place the supporting points a–g from Exercise 4 on page 52. What is the advantage of this plan?

Introduction:	The Internet can affect how we relate to friends, family, and colleagues in both positive and negative ways
Body paragraph 1:	Effects on family relationships
Evidence for negative effect:	
Evidence for positive effect:	
Body paragraph 2:	Effects on friendships
Evidence for negative effect:	
Evidence for positive effect:	
Body paragraph 3:	Effects on work relationships
Evidence for negative effect:	
Evidence for positive effect:	
Conclusion:	The internet can bring people together if used in the right way

Developing a paragraph

6 Study the Task 2 essay question below. The candidate has written the introductory paragraph and notes a–i on page 54 for the question. Complete the body of the essay by following steps 1–3.

1 Write G next to the notes which can be expanded to form general statements and S next to the notes which give specific supporting information.
2 Arrange the notes in a logical order. Think about the best sequence of general statements and make sure that each is followed by one or two supporting details.
3 Write the essay, adding signposting expressions to emphasise main points and moderating statements when required.

> To what extent has information technology reduced inequality in countries with developed economies?

Introduction

People who live in countries with developed economies often take access to information technology for granted. They find it hard to imagine a world in which this technology does not bring greater prosperity for everyone. However, as the IT revolution moves forward, some people are left behind. Indeed, there are several barriers to wider IT access and its potential benefits.

a *in some areas, many adults have poor literacy*
b *basic infrastructure is not universally good*
c *the poor even struggle to pay for electricity*
d *lack of literacy skills is an obstacle*
e *people on low income cannot afford broadband*
f *broadband access lacking, especially in rural areas*
g *poverty is one aspect of the problem*
h *people and businesses affected by slow broadband*
i *older women and the poor more likely to have lower levels of literacy*

Part 3: Exam practice

WRITING TASK 1: Describe a table

You should spend about 20 minutes on this task.

> The table shows the average length of video advertisements on the Internet and the average length of time viewers spend watching them.
> Summarise the information by selecting and reporting the main features and make comparisons where relevant.

Write at least 150 words.

Average online video ad length and time viewed		
Type of advertisement	**Average length of advertisement (seconds)**	**Average time viewed (seconds)**
Public service	45.8	18.5
Automotive	27.2	14.7
Financial services	20.5	16.3
Travel	18.0	13.0
Entertainment	27.8	10.8
Home furnishings	17.3	10.0
Consumer electronics	15.3	7.1
Pharmaceuticals	16.6	6.3
Clothing	14.6	6.0
Other retail	21.0	4.5
Overall	**22.4**	**10.7**

WRITING TASK 2: Write an essay evaluating an idea

You should spend about 40 minutes on this task.

Write about the following topic:

> New technologies and ways of buying and selling are transforming the lives of consumers?
> To what extent do you agree or disagree with this opinion?
> Give reasons for your answer and include any relevant examples from your own knowledge or experience.

Write at least 250 words.

🎓 Exam tutor

1 What language can you use to highlight key points in Writing Tasks 1 and 2?

2 Which writing task generally requires more moderate language? Why?

3 How should you structure Task 1 body paragraphs?

4 For the Task 1 summary, do you need to include all of the information in the visual prompt?

5 For the Task 2 essay, what is the advantage of grouping points thematically?

7 Consumer spending

Language development | Personal finances and spending expressions; Using precise language
Exam skills | Task 1: Describing the relationship between two visual prompts; Expressing cause and effect relationships tentatively; Task 2: Signposting examples and supporting evidence; Developing a paragraph with examples and evidence
Exam practice | Task 1: Describe and compare a linear graph and set of pie charts
Task 2: Write an essay proposing a solution

Part 1: Language development

Personal finances and spending expressions

1 Match the photos 1–8 to the expressions a–h in the box.

a food and drink   b transportation   c clothing and footwear   d entertainment

e housing   f dining out   g utilities   h home furnishings

2 The words in the two boxes can be paired to form common collocations. Complete sentences 1–5 on page 57 by choosing one word from each box below.

consumer	debt
goods	expenditure
disposable	income
personal	confidence
household	services

1 _____ _____ is the amount of money left after you have paid for all of the things that you need.

2 Over the last two decades, many people spent more money than they earned, resulting in high levels of _____ _____.

3 Spending on _____ and _____ , such as clothing and financial advice has decreased because of the economic slowdown.

4 When people feel more secure in their jobs, _____ _____ grows and people begin to spend money more freely.

5 _____ _____ is another way of saying the amount of money each domestic unit spends.

3 The paragraph below is from an essay written in response to the Task 2 question:

How do people learn to manage their money? Complete the text with the words in the box.

| on credit | quantity | financial | criteria | behaviour | saved | costly |

From their early years, children can observe how their parents make (1) _____ decisions. They may notice, for example, whether money is (2) _____ for (3) _____ purchases, or whether purchases are bought (4) _____ . Children can also see what kinds of (5) _____ parents use when choosing what to buy, for instance, whether quality or (6) _____ is more important. It is important, therefore, that parents model sensible purchasing (7) _____ and explain what they are doing and why. However, in many circumstances, this may not be enough.

Using precise language

🔅 Exam tip

When speaking, we often use vague words such as *thing* or *stuff* because the context usually makes the meaning clear. In academic writing, you should use more precise terms wherever possible.

4 Replace the words in italics in sentences 1–6 with the expressions in the box.

| their necessities | their possessions | aspects of |
| products | take action | advantages |

1 People often buy *things*, even when they do not need them. _____
2 One of the interesting *things about* consumer behaviour is that it is often irrational. _____
3 People can *do things* to avoid getting into debt. _____
4 One of the *good things* about shopping online is the convenience. _____
5 Often people's income barely covers the cost of *the things that they need*. _____
6 People are often very attached to *the things that they own*. _____

Part 2: Exam skills

Task 1: Describing the relationship between two visual prompts

> ### *i* Exam information: Describing figures
> Writing Task 1 sometimes requires you to describe two or more figures. Before writing your response, consider the relationship between them.

1 Answer questions 1–4 in relation to the graph and table below.

    1 What do both figures relate to?

    2 What do you think the relationship might be between the trends shown in the line graph and the information in the table?

    3 Which aspects of each figure should you highlight in your response?

    4 Should you describe each figure separately or compare features of both figures in each paragraph?

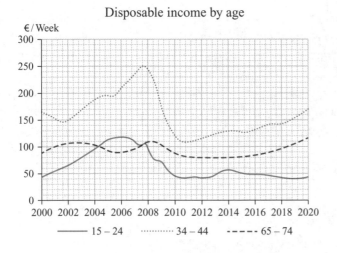

Disposable income by age

Percentage increase or decrease in sales

	2000 – 2004	2005 – 2009	2010 – 2014	2015 – 2020
Trainers	4%	−5%	1%	2%
Mobile phones	12%	6%	4%	4%
Home furnishings	3%	7%	−8%	2%
Skateboards	6%	−4%	2%	1%
Reading glasses	1%	−1%	0%	1%
Children's toys	3%	5%	2%	3%
Theatre tickets	1%	−2%	−2%	1%

2 Read the response below to the graph and table task on page 58 and answer questions 1–6.

The line graph shows average disposable income for three age groups from 2000 to 2020. The table gives the percentage increase in sales for seven products at five-year intervals from 2000 to 2020. Seen together, the figures suggest a link between age, disposable income and sales.

The disposable income of young people peaked in 2006 then fell sharply until 2010. After a slight recovery in 2014, it remained relatively flat thereafter. Sales of products typically enjoyed by young people, trainers, mobile phones, and skateboards, showed a similar pattern with sales of these products growing strongly between 2000 and 2004 (4%, 12% and 6% respectively).

The disposable income of the 35-44 age group peaked in 2008, fell steeply until 2010, then increased gradually. Sales of home furnishings and children's toys – items that people of this age group might buy - also peaked between 2005 and 2009, with particularly strong growth in furniture sales (7%).

For people aged 65-74, disposable income remained roughly constant. Not surprisingly, sales of reading glasses and theatre tickets also remained relatively steady throughout the period.

Overall, the figures suggest that the sales performance of different types of products may be influenced by the disposable income available to different sectors of the population.

1 What information is given in each sentence of the introduction?
2 What type of relationship between the two figures is identified and how is this expressed?
3 How is each of the three body paragraphs structured?
4 What specific information has the writer chosen to highlight? Why?
5 What expressions has the writer used to highlight the similarities in the trends represented?
6 What expression is used in the conclusion to express the relationship between the two figures?

Expressing cause and effect relationships tentatively

3 Study the graph and the bar chart below. Then rephrase sentences 1 and 2 twice using the expressions in the boxes.

1 The two figures show that there is a *positive correlation* between the availability of cheap credit and levels of consumer spending.

> when ... rises, ... also appear to ...   the more ... the more ...

2 The two figures show that the rate of taxation *correlates negatively* with levels of consumer spending.

> when ... falls, ... appear to ...   the less ... the more ...

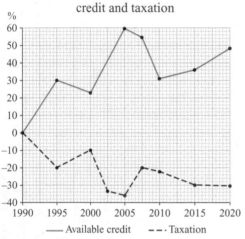

Figure 1: Percentage change in consumer credit and taxation

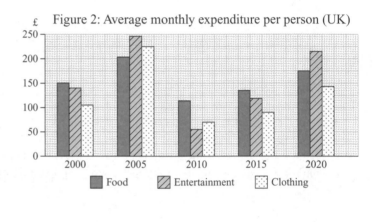

Figure 2: Average monthly expenditure per person (UK)

4 Write a description of the two figures in Exercise 3 using the following prompts.

Introduction:	• State what figure 1 shows.
	• State what figure 2 shows.
Body paragraph 1:	• Describe the overall relationship between the availability of credit and consumer spending using one of the phrases from Exercise 3.
	• Give a more detailed description of the trends.
Body paragraph 2:	• Describe the overall relationship between taxation and consumer spending using one of the phrases from Exercise 3.
	• Give a more detailed description of the trends.
Conclusion:	• Rephrase the relationship between credit, taxation and spending.

Task 2: Signposting examples and supporting evidence

5 Study the Writing Task 2 question below. Compare the two responses and answer questions 1–5.

> What influences our purchasing decisions? Do we mainly buy things because we need them, or are other factors involved?

Response 1

Sometimes people are more likely to buy products because celebrities have been employed to advertise them. The famous people used in these advertisements make these products more attractive. People want to purchase them. The influence of celebrities can be a powerful reason for some purchasing decisions.

Response 2

Sometimes people are more likely to buy products because celebrities have been employed to advertise them. In buying the product, the consumer may feel 'closer' to a person they admire. This can be seen, for example, when famous sportsmen or women endorse a particular brand of trainer or sportswear. Indeed, the powerful influence of this type of advertising on consumer behaviour is reflected in the large sums of money such celebrities are often paid for their advertising work.

1 Which response do you think is more satisfactory? Why?
2 What is the purpose of the first sentence in Responses 1 and 2?
3 What is the purpose of each of the remaining sentences in Response 2?
4 What expression is used to signal that the writer is giving an example?
5 What expression is used to signal that the writer is supporting the main point with evidence?

6 Complete the text below with signpost expressions from the Exam tip below. There may be more than one correct answer for each space.

> It is often the case that consumers buy products on impulse simply because of the way they are displayed. In supermarkets, (1) _____, snacks are often situated by the checkout to tempt those who are tired and bored with queuing. (2) _____ is when necessities such as clothes are displayed with matching accessories, such as jewellery. (3) _____ shoppers are often surprised at how much more they spend than they had intended.

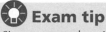 **Exam tip**

Signpost examples with phrases such as: *for example, an example of this, for instance*. To reinforce an idea, use *indeed, in fact*.

Developing a paragraph with examples and evidence

7 Develop each statement 1–3 below into a paragraph by giving examples and supporting evidence.

1 Some people buy products that they do not really need because they feel empty and unhappy.
2 People often buy products they do not really need because they want to display their status or wealth.
3 Sometimes people buy products they do not really need because they want to use them in a positive way to make their lives more enjoyable or interesting.

8 Read the Writing Task 2 question below and write a body paragraph about it. Remember to make a main point and to give examples to support your idea.

> The increased availability of consumer credit in some countries has contributed to the problem of debt. Who is responsible for high levels of indebtedness: the banks that lend money or the individuals who borrow money?

💡 Exam tip

Before writing a body paragraph, ask yourself:
- What main point do I want to make?
- What do I know that makes me want to say this?
- What would I say to persuade someone that my point is valid?
- How long should the paragraph be?

Part 3: Exam practice

WRITING TASK 1: Describe and compare a linear graph and set of pie charts

You should spend about 20 minutes on this task. Write at least 150 words.

> The figures give information about economic growth and household expenditure across a range of categories. Summarise the information by selecting and reporting the main features, and make comparisons where relevant.

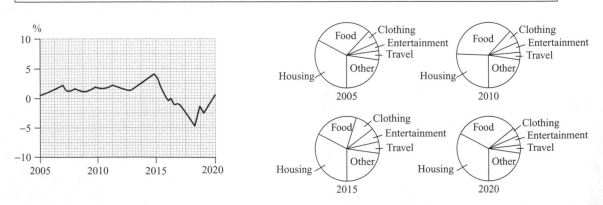

WRITING TASK 2: Write an essay proposing a solution

You should spend about 40 minutes on this task.

Write about the following topic:

Learning to manage money is one of the key aspects of adult life. How in your view can individuals best learn to manage their money?

Give reasons for your answer and include any relevant examples from your own knowledge or experience.

Write at least 250 words.

🎓 Exam tutor

1 What words and expressions have you learned for categories of items people commonly buy?

2 Why should you avoid using words like *thing* in the Writing exam?

3 When you have two or more visual prompts for Task 1, should you write about them separately?

4 What expressions can you use to express correlation?

5 What expressions can you use to signpost examples and emphasise main points?

8 Children and parents

Language development | Expressions related to age; Rights and responsibilities expressions
Exam skills | Task 1: Developing a paragraph with supporting details; Signalling supporting details; Task 2: Using modal verbs appropriately; Developing a conclusion
Exam practice | Task 1: Describe a bar chart; Task 2: Write an essay evaluating a solution

Part 1: Language development

Expressions related to age

1 Match the people a–e with the stages of life 1–5. Then order 1–5 from youngest to oldest on the line below.

a   adult
b   adolescent
c   infant
d   pensioner
e   child

1   old age
2   childhood
3   adolescence
4   adulthood
5   infancy

_____   _____   _____   _____   _____

youngest   oldest

Rights and responsibilities expressions

2 Decide which of the expressions a-j are rights (R) and which are responsibilities (RES).

a   be entitled to _____
b   have a duty to _____
c   be obliged to _____
d   be empowered to _____
e   be committed to _____

f   be allowed to _____
g   be authorised to _____
h   be permitted to _____
i   be required to _____
j   be held accountable for _____

3 Circle the correct option for the phrases in italics in sentences 1–5 that expresses the right or responsibility more strongly.

1 The children were *forced / obliged* to sit still throughout the lesson.
2 Adolescents appreciate being *allowed / empowered* to make their own decisions.
3 Often employees are *compelled / required* to retire when they reach the age of sixty-five.
4 Parents are *committed to doing / have a duty to do* their best for their children.
5 The young men were *required to join / coerced into joining* the army.

> **! Watch out**
>
> Abstract words such as *right* and *responsibility* have different meanings in different contexts.

4 Sentences 1–8 contain common set expressions requiring prepositions. Complete the sentences using the propositions in the box.

for	from	in	into	of	on	over	with

> **Exam tip**
>
> Some nouns, verbs and adjectives are commonly followed by certain prepositions, e.g. *believe **in***.

1 Parents sometimes don't have enough control _____ their children.
2 Young people often think their parents interfere too much _____ their lives.
3 It is better to discuss responsibilities _____ adolescents than to impose responsibilities _____ them.
4 Children must learn to cooperate _____ others in order to achieve goals.
5 In some countries the age _____ criminal responsibility is as low as twelve.
6 When setting standards _____ behaviour, the child's level of maturity should be taken _____ account.
7 In order for children to distinguish between right _____ wrong, they need to be held accountable _____ their actions.
8 Parents do not always behave _____ the best interests _____ their children.

5 Complete sentences 1–5 with expressions from Exercise 4.

1 It is unethical if professionals do not act _____ their clients.
2 If a child has a disability, this has to be _____ when deciding on a programme of education.
3 To work in a team, you have to demonstrate that you can _____.
4 When a government imposes too many regulations, people often complain that it is _____.
5 If managers _____ their employees, the employees might not take the initiative.

Part 2: Exam skills

Task 1: Developing a paragraph with supporting details

1 Study the table below that shows the results of a survey of 200 adolescents and their parents. Then compare the first paragraphs of two different responses to the survey and answer questions 1–2.

    1 Which response do you think is more satisfactory? Why?

    2 Why do you think the writer of Response 2 has chosen to include certain supporting details and not others?

Parents and adolescents' views of parental restrictions on adolescent decision-making

Parents should place restrictions on:	Fathers	Mothers	Adolescent girls	Adolescent boys
how adolescents spend their free time	72%	67%	23%	19%
what subject(s) they study	68%	58%	33%	49%
how they spend money they have earned	34%	23%	12%	9%
what occupation they pursue	55%	53%	18%	21%
what friends they make	76%	78%	17%	22%

Response 1

Overall, parents said that they wanted more control over their children than did the adolescents surveyed. For some decisions, the difference in opinion was quite large. In addition, fathers reported wanting more control than mothers over all except one of the choices. Boys were also prepared to accept more parental control than girls in four of the six choices.

Response 2

Overall, parents said that they wanted significantly more control over their children than did the adolescents surveyed. This is particularly evident in the issue of 'how adolescents spend their free time' and 'what friends they make'. Roughly three out of four parents wanted to place restrictions on these areas, whereas only one in five children felt this was needed. The biggest conflict of opinion concerned young people's choice of friends, with nearly 80 percent of mothers believing they should exercise control and only 17 percent of adolescent girls agreeing. The only area where there was some agreement among parents and young people was in restrictions on choice of subjects for study, selected by 58 percent of mothers and 49 percent of adolescent boys.

Signalling supporting details

2 Add the expressions in the box to the appropriate category 1–4 in the table.

in particular	for instance	the sole	such as
particularly	the most common		

Type of signal	Examples
1 superlatives	*the biggest difference*
2 expressions indicating example	*for example*
3 focusing expressions	*especially*
4 expressions indicating uniqueness	*the only*

3 Underline expressions that signal supporting detail in the Response 2 text on page 66. Indicate the types of signal in the text by using the categories 1–4 from the table above.

4 Complete the paragraph below with expressions from Exercise 2. There may be more than one correct answer.

Fathers generally reported wanting more control than mothers, the (1) _____ exception being control over what friends their children make, where 76% of fathers, as opposed to 78% of mothers, wanted a say. In addition to choice of friends, fathers were (2) _____ keen to exercise control over how adolescents spend their free time and what they studied. The (3) _____ gap between fathers' and mothers' views was over how children spend their self-earned money. Over a third of fathers wanted to place restrictions on this area, whereas only 23% of mothers wanted to do so.

5 Choose supporting detail from the table in Exercise 1 on page 66 to complete the paragraph below.

The adolescent boys surveyed also indicated a greater acceptance of parental control than did the adolescent girls ...

_____

_____

_____

_____

_____

_____

Task 2: Using modal verbs appropriately

6 Read the example Task 2 essay below that answers the question: *What can society do to ensure that the rights of young people are respected?* Match the modal verb forms 1–9 in the text with the functions a–e below.

a making a promise or prediction _____
b describing the possible consequence(s) of an action _____
c indicating strong obligation or necessity _____
d making a suggestion and indicating that an action is possible _____
e tentatively making a suggestion and indicating possibility _____

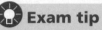 **Exam tip**
Modal verbs such as *can, should* and *might* help frame ideas in your writing. They are commonly used to indicate intention, obligation, permission, ability, and possibility.

In most countries around the world, children are recognised as persons by law. However, because children do not have the same access to power as adults, they lack the means to defend their rights. It is therefore important that adults recognise the rights of young people. Some argue that this is uniquely the duty of parents. In my view, society **(1)** *must* bear some of this responsibility. In this essay I **(2)** *will* outline three measures that can be taken to safeguard the rights of young people.

Firstly, government **(3)** *can* ensure that its policies take the interests of children into account. It **(4)** *could*, for example, appoint a children's commissioner to scrutinise new legislation for compliance with frameworks such as the UN Convention on the Rights of the Child. This **(5)** *would* ensure that young people are continuously represented in the halls of power.

Secondly, local government and charities **(6)** *can* ensure that young people have access to independent confidential sources of help. Telephone help lines are just one example of what **(7)** *could* be done. One such service in the UK, Childline, received over 700,000 calls last year, suggesting a strong need for this kind of help.

A third possible measure is to ensure that information about children's rights is widely disseminated through schools, for example, and the mass media. Children who are well-informed about their rights **(8)** *would* be in a better position to seek help to defend them.

In short, society has an obligation to look after young people. Doing so **(9)** *could* have benefits for all. Young people who have felt valued by society are more likely to recognise the value of society and behave accordingly.

7 Read the example Task 2 essay above again, then answer questions 1–3.

1 Which three modal verbs are used most frequently in the essay in Exercise 6? Why?
2 In what circumstances would you use the modal verb *should* instead of *must*?
3 When would you use *may*?

8 Read the partially completed Task 2 response to the question: *What can be done to encourage young people to become responsible members of society?*

Complete the text by adding a modal verb to the gaps 1–10. In some cases, more than one modal verb is possible – your choice will depend on how emphatic you wish to be.

In many societies these days, people are concerned about deteriorating standards of behaviour among young people. Petty crime, antisocial behaviour and apparent lack of respect for others all seem to be on the rise. Some people maintain that the best way to address this problem is to reinstate firm discipline within homes and schools. I (1) _____ suggest that although this (2) _____ be one solution, we (3) _____ approach the task of encouraging responsible behaviour among young people in a variety of ways.

One measure that both parents and teachers (4) _____ take is to involve young people in making decisions about what is acceptable behaviour. In schools for example, teachers (5) _____ draw up a contract with the children in their class. It (6) _____ need to be revised periodically as the children mature and are able to handle more freedom responsibly. Doing this (7) _____ discourage children from using misbehaviour as a means of expressing their independence.

Secondly, young people (8) _____ be taught leadership skills by taking part in organisations such as the Scouts. Young people who have experienced what it is like to be a leader (9) _____ probably have a better understanding of the difficulties involved. This (10) _____ encourage them to cooperate more easily with authority figures ...

Developing a conclusion

9 Read the three conclusions on page 70 to the Task 2 question in Exercise 8. Then match the features a–d to the numbered sections 1–5. Some of the features can be used more than once.

a restating your opinion _____

b summarising the main points _____

c making a recommendation _____

d make a prediction (often stating what may happen if the recommended action is or is not taken) _____

> **Exam tip**
>
> Conclusions to academic essays often contain standard features. Make sure you use these features in the Writing exam.

1 A more effective approach is to educate the public about the benefits of biodiversity. Efforts to research and develop the world's biological resources should be widely publicized. 2 Once people understand that there are real benefits to exploiting natural resources in a sustainable way, they are more likely to make the short-term sacrifices necessary to preserve natural habitats.

3 In brief, I do not believe it is possible to make recommendations regarding the supervision of adolescents that fit all contexts. 4 The physical environment, the cultural context, and the personalities of those involved should all be considered.

In short, there is little about today's celebrity culture that is fundamentally more harmful than the types of celebrity children have encountered in the past. 5 Provided children are given appropriate guidance, they are unlikely to be adversely affected.

10 Read the conclusion below that is from the text on page 68. Then answer questions 1–5.

In short, society has an obligation to look after young people. Doing so can have benefits for all. Young people who have felt valued by society are more likely to recognise the value of society and behave accordingly.

1 What expression is used to signal that this is the conclusion?
2 What other expressions can be used for this purpose?
3 Which of the functions a–d in Exercise 9 is used in the first sentence?

4 Which of the functions a–d in Exercise 9 is used in the second sentence?
5 How would you summarise the main points of the essay in a single sentence?

11 Complete the essay in Exercise 8 on page 69 by writing a conclusion. Write one sentence for each of the functions a–d listed in Exercise 9.

Part 3: Exam practice

WRITING TASK 1: Describe a bar chart

You should spend about 20 minutes on this task. Write at least 150 words.

The figure shows the results of a survey of 1000 adolescents in five different countries. The participants were asked at what age they believed certain rights and responsibilities should be granted to young people. Summarise the information by selecting and reporting the main features.

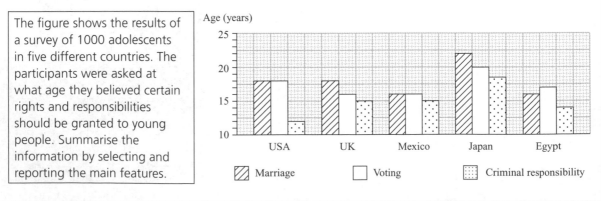

WRITING TASK 2: Write an essay evaluating a solution

You should spend about 40 minutes on this task. Write about the following topic:

In many countries, young people are granted certain privileges and responsibilities at the age of 16. Clearly parents have a responsibility to both care for and prepare their children as they approach this important milestone.

To what degree should parents intervene in the lives of their 15-year-old children?

Give reasons for your answer and include any relevant examples from your own knowledge or experience.

Write at least 250 words.

Exam tutor

1 Which expressions can be used to express rights?

2 What types of signalling expressions can you use to indicate that you are giving detailed information in support of a general point?

3 What are the different functions of modal verbs?

4 What are the different functions expressed by *can*?

5 What elements can you include in a Task 2 essay conclusion?

9 An ageing population

Part 1: Language development

Expressions related to people and places

1 Complete sentences 1–7 with words from the box. Use each word once.

> demographic boom census density accelerate generation elderly

1 Overpopulation relates not just to the size of the population but also to the _____ of population.
2 Many people predict that population growth will _____ over the next 30 years before levelling off at approximately 10 billion.
3 The 2011 _____ revealed that the average age of the population had risen considerably.
4 Governments regularly gather _____ data, including information about age, gender, income, and employment status, in order to plan effectively for the future.
5 The proportion of the population composed of children has declined, whereas the proportion of the population that is _____ has grown.
6 The recent jump in the numbers of people aged 60 to 65 in some countries can be attributed to the _____ in births after 1945.
7 People are concerned that caring for the elderly will be a burden for the younger _____.

Causes and consequences of an ageing population

2 Decide which of the expressions a–h refer to causes (C) and which refer to consequences (CON).

a increasing public health costs ____
b lower fertility rate ____
c decreasing mortality from infectious diseases ____
d increasing incidence of chronic illnesses ____

e growing pressure on care givers ____
f family planning ____
g dwindling pension funds ____
h improved health care ____

3 Complete sentences 1–7 with expressions from Exercise 2 on page 72. Make any changes necessary.

1 The increasing numbers of older people has put _____, especially women in their 40s.
2 _____ have been a cause for concern among governments and companies and have led to calls for the working population to save more for retirement.
3 _____ has resulted not only in greater longevity but also in better health among the elderly.
4 _____ such as cholera and polio has been a welcome development.
5 As the population ages, there has been an _____ and diabetes.
6 Unless measures are taken to reduce _____, these will result in higher taxes.
7 _____ measures have undoubtedly reduced birth rates in some countries.

Cohesive devices

4 Match each type of cohesive device a–e in the box with the examples in the table.

a coordinating conjunctions, e.g. *and*, *but*, *or*
b pronouns, e.g. *he*, *she*, *it*
c subordinating conjunctions, e.g. *when*, *whereas*, *although*
d relative pronouns, e.g. *who*, *whose*, *where*
e conjunctive adverbs e.g. *therefore*, *furthermore*, *consequently*

Exam tip

In the exam, you need to write coherently, link points within a sentence and between sentences. You can do this using a range of cohesive devices.

Device	Short sentences	Linked or combined sentences
1 ___	a Many people enjoy retirement. b Many people find they have the time for activities they enjoy.	Many people enjoy retirement. *They* find they have the time for activities they enjoy.
2 ___	a Lower mortality is due to increased longevity. b Increased longevity results from improved health care.	Lower mortality is due to increased longevity, *which* results from improved health care.
3 ___	a There are more jobs opportunities in cities. b People migrate to cities from rural areas.	There are more jobs opportunities in cities, *so* people migrate to them from rural areas.
4 ___	a Couples are under pressure to work. b Couples often delay starting a family.	*Because* couples are under pressure to work, they often delay starting a family.
5 ___	a People want to enjoy retirement. b People do not always save enough for a comfortable retirement.	People want to enjoy retirement; *however*, they do not always save enough for a comfortable retirement.

Part 2: Exam skills

Task 1: Correcting punctuation

1 Read the text that features the sentences from Exercise 4 and circle the punctuation marks. Notice how each cohesive device is punctuated. Then answer questions 1–4.

! Watch out

Accurate use of cohesive devices requires a good understanding of punctuation.

> Many people enjoy retirement. *They* find they have the time for activities they enjoy.
>
> Lower mortality is due to increased longevity, *which* results from improved health care.
>
> There are more jobs opportunities in cities, *so* people migrate to them from rural areas.
>
> *Because* couples are under pressure to work, they often delay starting a family.
>
> People want to enjoy retirement; *however*, they do not always save enough for a comfortable retirement.

1 What type of punctuation should you use with coordinating conjunctions?
2 When should you use a semicolon (;)?
3 Do you always have to use a comma with relative pronouns?
4 Do you always have to use a comma with subordinating conjunctions?

2 Make four corrections to punctuation in the Task 1 paragraph below.

> *The graph illustrates two contrasting trends. Whereas the proportion of the world's population aged 65 and above is expected to rise the proportion of those under five is expected to decline. The proportion of elderly people has risen gradually from approximately 5% in 1950 to roughly 7.5% today and over the next 30 years it is expected to more than double. However the proportion of young children has fallen gradually since 1970 from approximately 14% to 9%. It is forecast to continue falling at roughly the same rate until 2040. When it will level off.*

Improving a paragraph by combining sentences

3 Combine sentences 1–4 below into one paragraph, using a range of cohesive devices. Make any changes necessary and punctuate each sentence correctly.

1 The bar chart shows the percentage of males and females. The males and females were over the age of 65 in 2000.
2 Korea, Mexico, and Turkey are all developing or newly industrialized countries. Korea, Mexico, and Turkey are expected to experience large increases in the proportion of the population that is elderly.
3 The biggest increase is likely to occur in Korea. The proportion of pensioners in Korea is expected to increase from 10% to 35%.
4 The changes in all three countries will occur from a relatively low base. The predicted proportion of elderly residents will still be lower than that expected in developed economies.

Removing unnecessary words

4 Improve the paragraph below by removing unnecessary cohesive devices, dividing sentences that are too complex, and correcting the punctuation.

The figure shows the distribution of the population in terms of gender and age, and in fact, the age group with the highest percentage of both men and women is 55 to 59. Moreover, roughly five percent of the population is in this age group. In addition, the age groups with the next highest proportion of the population are 30 to 34 and 35 to 39. Also, it is interesting that until the age of 59, the proportion of males and females is roughly equal, however, thereafter, women make up a higher proportion of the elderly population and this trend is particularly evident in those aged 80. For example, over four percent of women fall into in this category. Whereas only two percent of men have reached this age.

> ### 💡 Exam tip
> Use linking words such as *moreover* when you are emphasising an additional point. Use words such as *although* or *however* to indicate contrasting ideas.

Task 2: Creating cohesion with summary words

5 Look at the essay extracts below from sample responses you have seen in previous units. Link the sentences by filling in the gaps with appropriate summary words.

> ### 💡 Exam tip
> Cohesion is often maintained by *this* or *these* + a summary word referring to the main point of the preceding sentence, e.g. *The gap in life expectancy has grown.* **This trend** *is likely to continue.*

1 *The changes that result from allowing men into female-dominated occupations and vice versa may be subtle, but they are far-reaching. However, to benefit the most from this _____, it is important not to expect males and females to approach work in identical ways.*

2 *However, exams also have clear drawbacks. Test-wise candidates can often perform well on exams without having good underlying knowledge or skills. On the other hand, some test-takers perform poorly on exams simply because of anxiety. Some teachers and learners focus only on those aspects of the curriculum that are likely to be tested, thus narrowing the educational experience for all. A number of measures should be taken to address these _____.*

3 *Governments could promote greater understanding of plants and animals by investing in the research and preservation efforts of universities, zoos and botanical institutes... However, this _____ alone would do little to protect whole ecosystems that are under threat.*

4 *It is true that as the balance of power among groups of people throughout history has shifted, languages have arisen, changed, and died out. Even once widely spoken languages, such as Latin, have disappeared. To some extent, therefore, this _____ may be inevitable.*

6 Read the passage below and answer questions 1–5.

1 Which sentence conveys the main idea of the text?
2 Which key word has the writer repeated in order to make the organisation of the passage clear?
3 In which sentences does this repetition occur?
4 What words and expressions has the writer used to avoid repeating the word *pensioners*?
5 What words and expressions has the writer used to avoid repeating the word *funds*?

As the population ages, people can expect to spend a longer proportion of their lives as pensioners. The quality of life among older people has, therefore, become a focus of attention. A number of measures can be taken to ensure that the elderly can enjoy life after retirement.

One of the most important measures is to make sure the people of working age are setting aside enough funds for when they retire. This could be done through a government scheme such as the national insurance system in the UK, through employer contributions, or through compulsory private pension plans. Saving sufficient sums of money would ensure that the burden of looking after elderly people does not fall entirely to the younger generation. However, savings alone would probably be insufficient to guarantee a good retirement for all.

Another measure that should be taken is to invest properly in the health care services so that they are able to cope with the demands of an increasingly frail section of the population ...

Repetition and synonyms

7 Look at the Task 2 question and the sample response extract below. Notice how the key word *obligation(s)* is repeated. Write synonyms for the expressions *younger family members* and *older relations* in the spaces.

> What are the obligations of younger family members towards older relations?

In most societies, adults in their prime are expected to care for those who are becoming frailer due to old age. How one defines the specific responsibilities of younger family members towards older relations, however, depends on a number of factors, for example, the family's resources and the degree of state support available. Nevertheless, I would suggest a number of core obligations can be identified.

The most fundamental obligation that (younger family members) _____ have towards (older relations) _____ is to ensure that their physical needs are being met. It is particularly important that (older relations) _____ have good nutrition, adequate healthcare and a safe and warm environment. Whether this is provided in the family home or in an institution such as a nursing home does not matter.

Another core obligation is to ensure that (older relations) _____ continue to feel a sense of love and belonging. Whenever possible, they should be included in family occasions such as birthdays, weddings and funerals. Their value to the family as a whole should be acknowledged even if they are no longer able to contribute actively to the family, financially or otherwise.

Finally, (younger family members) _____ should ensure that (older relations) _____ continue to have the opportunity to grow and develop as individuals. As the process of personal development is never complete, people continue to need stimulation in the form of activities and interests throughout their lives. Reading aloud, watching a film together or playing a board game are all things that (younger family members) _____ can do with their (older relations) _____.

In short, ...

8 Look again at the first paragraph from the essay in Exercise 7. Underline the words and phrases that have opposite or contrasting meanings. The first example has been done for you.

In most societies, adults <u>in their prime</u> are expected to care for those who are <u>becoming frailer</u> due to old age. How one defines the specific responsibilities of younger family members towards older relations, however, depends on a number of factors, for example, the family's resources and the degree of state support available. Nevertheless, I would suggest a number of core obligations can be identified.

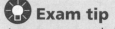 **Exam tip**

Antonyms are words that have the opposite meaning of another word, e.g, *large* and *small*, *old* and *young*. Antonyms are useful for structuring a text.

9 Now look at the Task 2 questions below. For each question, circle a key word that you might want to repeat, and underline any words or expressions which could be replaced with synonyms.

1 With improvements in life expectancy, people living today are clearly able to work productively for much longer than in the past. What are the arguments for and against a mandatory retirement age?

2 What are the most significant consequences of population ageing?

Topic sentences

10 Read the three topic sentences which open the three body paragraphs of the response to the Task 2 question on page 77. Underline the word or phrase in each that signals it is a topic sentence. Circle the phrase that expresses the main idea developed in the paragraph.

1 The most fundamental obligation that younger family members have towards older relations is to ensure that their physical needs are being met.
2 Another core obligation is to ensure that older relations continue to feel a sense of love and belonging.
3 Finally, younger family members should ensure that older relations continue to have the opportunity to grow and develop as individuals.

11 Write topic sentences for three paragraphs in response to the Task 2 question below. Then expand the first topic sentence into a paragraph. Make your paragraph cohesive using *this* (or *these*) + a summary word.

What are the most significant consequences of population aging?

Part 3: Exam practice

WRITING TASK 1: Describe a line graph

You should spend about 20 minutes on this task.

The figure shows demographic trends in an industrialized country.
Summarise the information by selecting and reporting the main features.

Write at least 150 words.

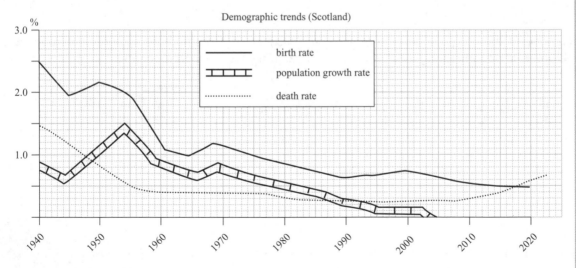

WRITING TASK 2: Write an essay discussing ideas

You should spend about 40 minutes on this task.

Write about the following topic:

> Longer life spans and improvements in the health of older people suggest that people over the age of 65 can continue to live full and active lives.
> In what ways can society benefit from the contribution that older people can make?

Give reasons for your answer and include any relevant examples from your own knowledge or experience.

Write at least 250 words.

🎓 Exam tutor

1 In what three ways could you combine these sentences? *People know they are going to grow older. People often do not prepare adequately for old age.*

2 Why is it more important to use words such as *however* to signal contrasting ideas than to use words such as *moreover* when adding a further point?

3 Where in an essay would you normally place the thesis statement?

4 What is the relationship between the thesis statement and topic sentences?

5 Why is it acceptable to repeat key words in a Task 2 essay?

10 Fame

Language development | Expressions related to popular culture; Expressing attitude with adverbs; Modifying adverbs
Exam skills | Task 1: Commonly confused words; Using formal language; Using synonyms to avoid repetition; Task 2: Choosing the right level of formality
Exam practice | Task 1: Describe a table; Task 2: Write about an opinion

Part 1: Language development

Expressions related to popular culture

1 Match the words 1–9 with the words a–i that have a similar meaning.

1	fame	a	short-lived
2	ambition	b	icon
3	achievement	c	accomplishment
4	shortcoming	d	approve
5	idol	e	stardom
6	transient	f	aspiration
7	endorse	g	notorious
8	image	h	flaw
9	infamous	i	impression

2 Complete the phrases in italics in sentences 1–6 with words from Exercise 1 to form common expressions. Make any necessary changes to the forms.

1 When you meet someone for the first time, it's important to *make a good _____* .
2 When starting a new project, it is common to be full of *hopes and _____*.
3 Many people see celebrities as being all *_____ and no substance*.
4 People often migrate to cities to seek *_____ and fortune*.
5 He has had big problems with his co-stars in the past, so his character must be *deeply _____*.
6 She aspired to becoming a *fashion _____* .

3 Arrange the groups of words below from left to right, according to strength of meaning.

1 famous   legendary   well-known
2 bad   imperfect   worthless
3 like   admire   idolise
4 praise   acclaim   recognition
5 brief   fleeting   transient

> **Exam tip**
>
> Some words have similar meanings but vary in strength, e.g. *satisfactory, good, excellent*. Make sure you use the words correctly.

Expressing attitude with adverbs

> **Exam tip**
>
> To express your opinion without using personal pronouns, use an attitude adverb at the beginning of your statement, rather than: *I think it's great that some celebrities are good role models.*, write: *Fortunately, some celebrities are good role models.*

4 Start each sentence 1–7 with an adverb from the box that expresses the attitude in brackets.

> fortunately   importantly   inevitably   interestingly
> obviously   surprisingly   unfortunately

1 _____, many people who achieve fame as children have difficulty living a normal adult life. (This is not a good thing.)
2 _____, some people who become famous as children go on to live very ordinary lives as adults. (This phenomenon is bound to happen.)
3 _____, only a small percentage of people become truly obsessed with celebrities. (This is a good thing.)
4 _____, the vast majority of respondents were critical of the amount of celebrity coverage in the news. (I didn't expect this.)
5 _____, fame can bring certain advantages. (This is clear.)
6 _____, the majority of children surveyed said that they did not want to be famous. (I find this interesting.)
7 _____, many children were critical of the bad behaviour of people in the public eye. (This idea is significant.)

Modifying adverbs

5 Complete sentences 1–4 with an adverb and a suitable modifier (*more, less, not, somewhat.*)

1 _____, fame can be stressful. (This is not as clear as the previous point.)
2 _____, the majority of children said they did not want to emulate the bad behaviour of their idols. (This idea is more significant than the previous one.)
3 _____, people find notorious criminals quite fascinating. (This is to be expected.)
4 _____, the children of famous people rarely seek fame themselves. (This is a bit surprising.)

Part 2: Exam skills

Task 1: Commonly confused words

Watch out

Some words that sound or look similar have different meanings, e.g. *principal vs principle*.

1 Sentences 1–6 describe information in the table below. Each sentence contains two commonly confused words in italics. Underline the correct word.

Children's career aspirations in 1990 and 2019

rank	1990	%	2019	%
1	Teacher	14	Sports star	20
2	Businessperson	9	Teacher	11
3	Doctor/nurse	8	Actor	7
4	Scientist	7	Video game designer	6
5	Police officer	6	Policeman/woman	5
6	Vet	6	Singer	5
7	Sports star	5	Doctor/nurse	4
8	Astronaut	4	Scientist	4
9	Banker	4	Vet	3
10	Archaeologist	3	Chef	2

1 Children today appear to have a greater interest in careers associated with celebrities than did children in the *passed / past*.
2 There were changes in the rankings of all of the occupations *accept / except* that of police officer.
3 The percentage of children choosing sports star as one of their top ten careers *rose / raised*.
4 In 2019, a higher proportion of children wanted to work in entertainment *then / than* in more traditional professions such as medicine.
5 *In contrast / On the contrary,* a much higher percentage of those surveyed selected sports star, which occupies first position in the 2019 list.
6 Some professions that did not appear in the 1990 rankings, *feature / future* prominently in the 2019 list.

2 Complete sentences 1–5 with some of the words in italics from Exercise 1.

1 The percentage of children wanting to be a sports star _____ significantly.
2 In 1990, teaching was a more popular career choice _____ medicine.
3 A smaller percentage of children today want to work in science than they did in the _____.
4 Not surprisingly, banker did not _____ in the 2019 list.
5 All of the professions in the 1990 list appeared in the 2019 list, _____ businessperson, astronaut, banker and archaeologist.

Using formal language

3 The paragraph below contains six informal expressions in italics. Replace them with more formal words or expressions.

There were (**1**) *really big* changes in the children's career aspirations between 1990 and 2020. (**2**) *Lots of* traditional professions either declined in popularity or disappeared. (**3**) *E.g.* in 1990, eight percent of respondents wanted to be doctors or nurses, whereas thirty years later, only four percent of those surveyed chose these professions. (**4**) *Amazingly*, businessperson, ranked second in 1990, (**5**) *didn't* even (**6**) *show up* in the top ten occupations of 2020.

1 _____   4 _____

2 _____   5 _____

3 _____   6 _____

Using synonyms to avoid repetition

Exam tip

It can be challenging to avoid repeating the same words and phrases in Task 1 summaries because of the way the information is presented. Learn synonyms for common expressions.

4 The passage below contains some unnecessary repetition of the words in bold. Replace the words 1–6 in italics with synonyms from Exercise 1 on page 82. Make any other necessary changes to the words.

A number of **professions** typically associated with celebrities, which were not included in the 1990 list, **appeared** among the top ten in 2020. Acting and singing were particularly popular, ranking third and sixth respectively. Chef, **chosen** by two percent of **respondents**, also (**1**) *appeared* in the 2010 list. Other (**2**) *professions* increased significantly in popularity. The percentage of (**3**) *respondents* (**4**) *choosing* sports star more than doubled. The only (**5**) *profession* that did not change in the rankings was police officer, which (**6**) *appeared* in fifth place in both 1990 and 2019.

1 _____   4 _____

2 _____   5 _____

3 _____   6 _____

5 The table below shows the results of an opinion poll. Read the description and circle the most appropriate option in the items 1–7 in italics. Then underline the expressions the writer has used to avoid repeating the word *respondents*.

Opinion poll of media coverage

Too much coverage of:	%	Too little coverage of:	%
Celebrity gossip	42	Good news	18
Politics	10	Poverty	11
Conflict	9	Environment	10
Crime	8	Education	9
The economy	8	Health	8
Sports	5	International news	4

The table presents the findings of a public opinion survey of media coverage.

On the whole, the respondents felt there was too much coverage of individuals in the entertainment industry and politics, 'bad' news and sports. Dissatisfaction with the amount of coverage given to celebrity gossip was particularly high at 42 percent. Individuals in politics were also seen as **(1)** *receiving / getting* too much attention by one in ten of those surveyed. A similar **(2)** *number / percentage* of respondents said the media focused too much on **(3)** *terrible / negative* news stories, conflict and the recession, for example. At the other end of the scale, a **(4)** *small / few* percentage of people questioned said there was too much sports news.

(5) *On the contrary / On the other hand*, respondents said that there **(6)** *wasn't / was not* enough coverage of good news, social and issues and international news. Nearly one in five of those who took part in the survey felt that there was not enough focus on good news. A relatively high percentage also felt that there was too little coverage of issues relating to quality of life: poverty, the environment, education and health. A small percentage (4%) wanted more international news.

In short, **(7)** *there appears to be / you could say there was* a mismatch between the types of news stories covered and the stated preferences of the survey respondents.

Task 2: Choosing the right level of formality

> ### ℹ Exam information: General v specialist knowledge
> Task 2 questions usually require you to discuss ideas or problems that require general rather than specialist knowledge, so the language required for IELTS Writing Task 2 is often predictable.

6 Listed below are ten common expressions. Write one or two words with a similar meaning for each.

1 advantage _____
2 disadvantage _____
3 opinion _____
4 however _____
5 people _____

6 problem _____
7 solution _____
8 important _____
9 issue _____
10 situation _____

7 Study the four introductions a–d to an essay written in response to the question: *In your view, why have celebrities become such an important feature of modern life?* Then answer questions 1–2.

1 Which is the best introduction?
2 What is the problem with each of the other three?

a

There are more and more television programmes, magazines, and newspaper articles about celebrities these days. The 'cult of celebrity' is one of the one of the things about modern pop culture that really stands out. Some people say that because there have always been famous people around, this isn't anything new. But I say that there's something different about fame today.

b

The number of television programmes, magazines, and newspaper articles focusing on the lives of celebrities has rocketed over the last few decades. Indeed, the 'cult of celebrity' is the defining feature of modern popular culture. People say that, because there have always been famous people, this is not a new phenomenon. However, I strongly believe that fame today is unique to our times.

c

The number of television programmes, magazines, and newspaper articles focusing on the lives of celebrities appears to have grown considerably over the last few decades. Indeed, the 'cult of celebrity' seems to be one of the defining features of modern popular culture. Some people insist that, because there have always been famous people, this is not a new phenomenon. However, I would suggest that there are aspects of fame today that are particular to our times.

d

The number of television programmes, magazines, and newspaper articles focusing on the lives of celebrities appears to have grown considerably over the last few decades. Indeed, the 'cult of celebrity' seems to be one of the defining features of television programmes, magazines and newspapers. Some people insist that, because there have always been famous people, the' cult of celebrity' is not a new phenomenon. However, I would suggest that there are aspects of the 'cult of celebrity' that are particular to our times.

8 Read the first two body paragraphs of the essay on page 85. Improve the text by:

    1 changing the informal expressions into more formal language.
    2 modify the statements 1–5 that are too emphatic by adding hedging expressions. Use the hints to help you.

Exam tip

Academic style usually avoids language that is informal or too emphatic. Use 'hedges' such as *sometimes, often, could* + verb to moderate your statements.

In the past, people (1) _____ became famous for doing great things. Einstein, Dickens, and Gandhi, for instance, were all celebrated for what they'd done for science, literature and public life. People were interested in them (2) _____ because they were role models.

One of the reasons fame today is so different is because celebrities (3) _____ satisfy a range of people's emotional needs, not just the need for role models. Lots of people in the public eye today are famous simply for being famous. The public are (4) _____ interested in them because, when news of scandals comes out into the open, they (5) _____ get the satisfaction of feeling superior to people they envy.

Add a hedge to show that this is a generalisation.

Add a hedge to show that this is not the only reason.

Add a hedge to indicate that this seems to be what happens.

Add a hedge to indicate that this doesn't happen all of the time.

Add a hedge that indicates this is a possibility.

9 Read the third body paragraph and the conclusion to the essay. Reduce the unnecessary repetition in the text by replacing repeated words with synonyms.

Another reason fame today is unique is the desire of ordinary people to explore the nature of fame itself. Many celebrities that have achieved fame through the Internet, for example, come from the same backgrounds as ordinary people. Watching such celebrities allows ordinary people to imagine what it might be like to suddenly find themselves in the public eye. Celebrities may, therefore, allow ordinary people to enjoy wish fulfilment fantasies without having to worry about whether they are capable of significant achievement.

The third and perhaps most significant reason that celebrities play such an important role in modern life is the fact that commercial pressures encourage media organisations to focus on information that is immediately attractive to ordinary people. As we have seen, celebrities appear to tap into powerful emotional needs: the need to feel superior, the need to imagine oneself to be the centre of attention; therefore, news about celebrities sells.

Watch out

If you do not know suitable synonyms for a key term, it is better to repeat the word rather than to use an unsuitable alternative.

Part 3: Exam practice

WRITING TASK 1: Describe a table

You should spend about 20 minutes on this task. Write at least 150 words.

The table shows the results of a survey of people's perception of celebrity news coverage. Summarise the information by selecting and reporting the main features, and make comparisons where relevant.

How much news coverage do celebrities receive?	%	Who is responsible for the amount of coverage?	%	Who gives celebrities the most coverage?	%
Too much	85	News organisations	56	Internet news websites	60
Not enough	6	The public	34	Television news	15
Right amount	7	Both	7	Newspapers	12
Don't know	2	Don't know	3	Radio news	5
				Other	3
				Don't know	5

WRITING TASK 2: Write about an opinion

You should spend about 40 minutes on this task. Write about the following topic:

Many people believe that media coverage of celebrities is having a negative effect on children.
To what extent do you agree or disagree with this opinion?

Give reasons for your answer and include any relevant examples from your own knowledge or experience.

Write at least 250 words.

🎓 Exam tutor

1 How can you express your personal opinion about an issue without using expressions such as *I believe, in my opinion*?

2 If you want to avoid repeating a word, why shouldn't you simply choose another word that sounds similar?

3 What sort of themes are found in Task 2 essays?

4 What is the difference in tone between academic language and everyday language?

5 What kind of words can you use to make a statement less emphatic?

11 Transportation

Language development | Expressions associated with transport; Word formation and parts of speech
Exam skills | Task 1: Correcting errors in verb forms and articles; Task 2: Correcting errors in sentence structure; Punctuation and linking; Proofreading your work
Exam practice | Task 1: Describe a table; Task 2: Write an essay proposing solutions

Part 1: Language development

Expressions associated with transport

1 Match the phrases a–h in the box with the road signs 1–8 above.

> **a** cycle route ahead   **b** pedestrian crossing ahead   **c** end of motorway   **d** traffic congestion likely
> **e** road works ahead   **f** danger ahead   **g** bus lane   **h** speed cameras in the area

2 Use the relevant words from the expressions in Exercise 1 to complete sentences 1–7.
 1 Unless we add new _____, the number bike journeys won't increase.
 2 Although _____ reduce the amount of road accidents, drivers don't like being under surveillance.
 3 Faulty traffic lights and poor road crossings put the lives of _____ in _____.
 4 Motorists will experience _____ on the roads during peak travel periods.
 5 _____ make travelling long distances faster but some people think they spoil the landscape.
 6 The upgrading of the road network means that journeys are delayed because of _____.
 7 The number of journeys by public transport increased when the government invested in _____ and more spacious buses.

Word formation and parts of speech

3 Complete the table below with the correct word forms.

verb	noun
_____	reduction
_____	production
convert	_____
maintain	_____
_____	emission
combust	_____
propel	_____

Exam tip

Academic writing requires a good knowledge of abstract nouns. Notice that the nouns in Exercise 3 all end in: –tion, –sion, or –ance. Another common ending for nouns is –ment.

4 Use words from Exercise 3 to complete the passage below. Make any changes necessary.

Electric cars are battery-powered vehicles (1) _____ by electric motors. Because electric cars are more efficient at (2) _____ stored energy into (3) _____ they have the potential to (4) _____ CO_2 emissions. The level of reduction depends on how the electricity is generated; however, it can be substantial. In the UK, for example, if vehicles with internal (5) _____ engines were replaced with electric vehicles, CO_2 (6) _____ would decrease by 40 %.

Moreover, because electric cars do not (7) _____ exhaust fumes, they have the potential to reduce urban pollution. Another advantage of electric cars is their low (8) _____ costs; because electric motors have fewer moving parts than petrol-powered engines, they are easier to maintain. One disadvantage, however, is that they (9) _____ less noise and can therefore be dangerous to pedestrians.

Governments and manufacturers around the world are investing substantial sums in the development of state-of-the-art electric cars and batteries. Some have predicted that electric car (10) _____ will increase substantially over the next decade and that by 2030, 20 % of cars on the road will be battery-powered.

5 Write the noun form of the verbs a–g. Use the endings –tion, –sion, –ance, or –ment and make any other changes necessary to the root form of the word.

a achieve _____
b appear _____
c allow _____
d explain _____
e involve _____
f provide _____
g oppose _____

6 Complete sentences 1–7 with the correct noun form from Exercise 5.

1 The local authority couldn't enforce the new parking restrictions because of public _____.
2 For many people, learning to dive is a significant _____.
3 The train operator couldn't offer a coherent _____ for why the train was late.
4 When purchasing a new car, people will often consider functionality, price and _____.
5 The new public transport scheme is unlikely to go ahead unless there is substantial financial _____ from government.
6 It is important that drivers make _____ for cyclists on busy roads.
7 Attempts to create pedestrian-only zones in cities won't succeed without the _____ of local businesses.

Part 2: Exam skills

Task 1: Correcting errors in verb forms and articles

> ### 💡 Exam tip
> Task 1 responses often contain errors in verbs tense. Use the past tenses for actions completed in the past, the present perfect for time periods up to the present, and the simple present for general truths.

1 Complete sentences 1–6 with the correct form of the verb in brackets.

  1 Between 2010 and 2015, there _____ a substantial decrease in petrol prices. (be)
  2 Petrol prices _____ substantially since 2015. (rise)
  3 The figure shows that if the price of petrol _____ to rise over the next five years, fewer people will choose to drive. (continue)
  4 As a general rule, car use _____ positively with per capita income. (correlate)
  5 The percentage of households in the UK with access to a car _____ from 50 percent to 75 percent between 1975 and 2000. (increase)
  6 According to the graph, car use _____ substantially when the oil crisis began. (already rise)

2 Underline the correct active or passive form in italics in sentences 1–6.

  1 Sales of electric cars *decreased / were decreased* for approximately three years.
  2 Electric car sales *expect / are expected* to rise over the next ten years.
  3 Petrol consumption *correlates / is correlated* negatively with population density.
  4 Use of public transport *varied / was varied* in relation to income and average distance travelled per year.
  5 Public transport *accounted / was accounted* for only ten percent of journeys to work in 2015.
  6 When they *asked / were asked* why they were reluctant to buy an electric car, the majority of respondents cited the following factors: cost, maintenance and reliability.

> ### 💡 Exam tip
> When one verb is followed by another, the second verb can either be an infinitive or an *–ing* form (or in some cases, both). The correct form depends on the first verb. Check in a dictionary for example sentences.

3 Read the exam tip above then complete sentences 1–6 with the infinitive or the *-ing* form of the word in brackets.

  1 Three-quarters of the survey participants said that, whenever possible, they avoided _____ (drive) at peak times.
  2 People below the age of 25 tended _____ (use) public transport more regularly than those aged over 54.
  3 Consumers often postpone _____ (purchase) a new car during periods of economic uncertainty.
  4 Even significant discounts on new car models did not make prospective buyers _____ (change) their minds.
  5 More people would consider _____ (travel) by public transport if it were cheaper and more reliable.
  6 Most people said that they intended _____ (reduce) their car use in future.

4 Study sentences 1–5 in the table and match each sentence with the rule for article use (a–e) listed in the box. The first two sentences are examples.

a When referring to a single countable noun, use *a* if you mean *one* or *any*.
b Use *the* with ordinal numbers, e.g. *the second*.
c Use *the* with superlatives, e.g. *the biggest*.
d Use *the* with adjectives that represent a class of people, e.g. *the educated*.
e Use *the* with words that express uniqueness, e.g. *the sole*.

🔆 Exam tip
Another common error is the misuse of articles *a* and *the*. The rules of article use in English are complex. However, most mistakes can be avoided by following some basic guidelines.

Example sentences	General rule
Cars can be seen as status symbols. (no articles)	When you make generalisations about countable nouns, use the plural form with no article.
The car that I bought last year has already been repaired twice.	When referring to a single countable noun, use *the* if you mean a specific one.
1 **The** wealthy could afford cars while **the** poor travelled on foot.	
2 **The** only electric car costing less than £20,000 is now on the market.	
3 **The** least fuel-efficient cars on the market tend to be luxury models.	
4 Most people would buy **a** new car if they could afford one.	
5 **The** first electric cars were built in the nineteenth century.	

5 Read the Task 1 response below. Complete the text by adding articles *a* and *the*. Where no article is needed, write –.

(1) _____ bar chart gives information about modes of transport used by (2) _____ people living in (3) _____ rural areas and cities of different sizes. It shows (4) _____ annual distance travelled by car, bus, train and foot per person.

Overall, the distance travelled is inversely proportional to the size of conurbation. People living in large cities (over, 50,000 inhabitants) travelled less than those living in (5) _____ cities with fewer than 50,000 people and considerably less than those living in rural areas. Inhabitants of (6) _____ largest cities (over 500,000) travelled (7) _____ fewest miles (approximately 5,500). In contrast, people living in the countryside travelled nearly twice that distance each year.

This tendency was particularly evident in relation to car travel. For all of (8) _____ categories represented in the table, cars considerably outweighed other forms of transport. However, people living in (9) _____ rural area travelled nearly three times the distance (over 9,000 miles) by car as people living in (10) _____ large city. In fact, car use correlated negatively with the size of the conurbation.

Other modes of transport, on the other hand, showed (11) _____ opposite tendency. Inhabitants of larger cities tended to travel more by train and bus and on foot than people in less populated areas.

In short, city living appears to be more environmentally friendly, at least as far as distance and mode of transport is concerned.

Task 2: Correcting errors in sentence structure

6 Ten of the most common errors in found in Task 2 responses involve the errors a–j below. Sentences 1–10 each contain one of the errors a–j. Identify the type of error in each sentence and correct it.

a subject-verb agreement __   f relative clauses __
b articles: *a / an / the* __   g verb forms: modal / infinitive / gerund __
c countable vs. uncountable nouns __   h tenses __
d prepositions __   i run-on sentences __
e word class __   j sentence fragments __

1 The evidences show that wearing a seatbelt significantly reduces road accident fatalities.
2 In fact wearing a seatbelt is most important safety measure that can be taken.
3 The number of road accidents has declined last year.
4 It is illegally to drive without a license or car insurance.
5 The cost of insurance depends of several factors including age, experience and type of car.
6 Organisations such as the AA can to provide assistance to motorists who break down.
7 Many people which living in rural areas have no choice but to travel by car.
8 Buying a second-hand car is sometimes risky, inexperienced buyers can be easily cheated.
9 There is numerous examples of illegal practices in the second-hand motor trade.
10 Because the industry is poorly regulated and buyers are not always well-informed.

7 Connect the pairs of sentences 1–5 using the linking words given in brackets.

1 In many parts of the world, people now have greater access to cars. They often have more choice over where they live and work. (as)

_____

_____

2 Cities have become more sprawling. People have sought out the greater privacy and space afforded by suburban living. (because)

_____

_____

3 There are more vehicles, often travelling at greater speed. The streets are less hospitable to pedestrians. (as a consequence)

_____

_____

4 There has also been a decline in public transport. People have less day-to-day contact with other members of their community. (as a result)

_____

_____

5 Most people are very dependent on their cars. Most people do not want to give up their cars. (since)

_____

_____

Punctuation and linking

8 Correct the punctuation in sentences 1–6.

1 Although most people say they would use other forms of transport for short journeys in fact most car journeys are for distances of less than two miles.

2 Most people are reluctant to buy electric cars because of three main factors, cost, maintenance and reliability.

3 Some of those surveyed, said they had concerns about the distance electric cars could travel before having to be recharged.

4 Electric cars are more expensive than conventional cars, however their maintenance costs are lower.

5 One major Japanese car manufacturer which produces some of the most fuel-efficient petrol-powered cars has recently announced that it plans to invest more heavily in electric car technology.

6 Hybrid and electric cars produce fewer emissions but this may not result in a reduction in overall emissions. Because the growth in car ownership over the next 15 years is likely to accelerate.

9 The essay extract below contains two very short sentences, one sentence fragment, and three long sentences that are missing linking words. Revise the text by correcting the punctuation and choosing from the list of linking words in the box to connect the ideas. You will not have to use all the linking words.

although	as	because	however	as a consequence
since	therefore	whereas	which	while

In many parts of the world, people now have greater access to cars, they often have more choice over where they live and work. Cities have become more sprawling, people have sought out the greater privacy and space afforded by suburban living. There are more vehicles. Often travelling at greater speed. The streets are less hospitable to pedestrians. There has also been a decline in public transport, people have less day-to-day contact with other members of their community.

💡 Exam tip

Some linking words have more than one meaning: *since* can refer to time or reason, e.g. *He has been driving since he was twenty.* (time)
More people are cycling since travel costs are so high. (reason)
Also check in a dictionary for the different meanings of *as* and *while*.

Proofreading your work

10 Read the essay extract below written in response to the question: *What are the most significant negative consequences of the massive expansion of car ownership?* Find and correct as many of the errors as you can.

One of the factors that distinguishes developed from developing economies is mass car ownership. The cars undoubtedly have practical benefits for the individuals who own them. They allow for more flexible and autonomous travel. Like other consumer items, they can used to express individual taste and identity, however, they also clearly have a number of undesirable consequences.

One of these consequences is deteriorate in people's health. Urban pollution, which is largely caused by vehicle emissions, can exacerbate respiratory problems such as asthma. This health problems is more prevalent in cities, particularly among children and elderly.

Another consequence of car use is a decline in levels of physical activity and hence levels of fitness. Although this is partly a consequence of rising prosperity generally there is evident that car use is responsible for lower levels of cardiovascular fitness. The vast majority of car journeys are for less than two miles, that is, distances that can easily be covered on foot. In short, when the people own cars, they tend to walking less, thus removing a major means by which people maintain day-to-day fitness.

Part 3: Exam practice

WRITING TASK 1: Describe a table

You should spend about 20 minutes on this task. Write at least 150 words.

The table shows the percentage of journeys made by different forms of transport in four countries. The bar chart shows the results of a survey into car use.
Summarise the information by selecting and reporting the main features, and make comparisons where relevant.

Most cited reasons people travel to work by car (USA)

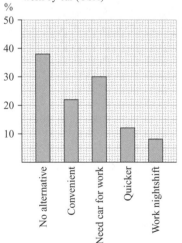

Journeys made by:	USA	UK	France	Netherlands
Car	90%	72%	68%	47%
Bicycle	1%	2%	2%	26%
Public transport	3%	12%	18%	8%
On foot	5%	11%	11%	18%
Other	1%	3%	1%	1%

WRITING TASK 2: Write an essay proposing solutions

You should spend about 40 minutes on this task.

Write about the following topic:

> There is a good deal of evidence that increasing car use is contributing to global warming and having other undesirable effects on people's health and well-being.
> What can be done to discourage people from using their cars?

Give reasons for your answer and include any relevant examples from your own knowledge or experience.

Write at least 250 words.

🎓 Exam tutor

1 How long should you spend on each writing task?

2 How many words should you write for each task?

3 What types of visual prompts are there for Task 1?

4 What do Task 2 questions normally require you to do?

5 What criteria will be used to assess your writing?

WRITING TASK 1

You should spend about 20 minutes on this task.

> The figure gives information about participation in seven common leisure activities.
>
> Summarise the information by selecting and reporting the main features, and make comparisons where relevant.

Write at least 150 words.

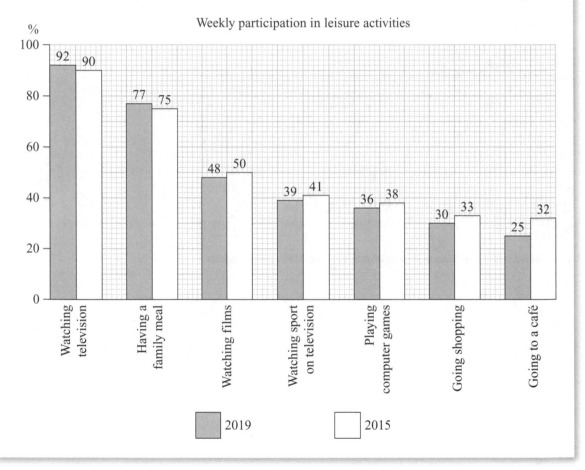

Weekly participation in leisure activities

WRITING TASK 2

You should spend about 40 minutes on this task.

Write about the following topic:

> In recent years, there has been growing interest in the relationship between inequality and personal achievement. Some people believe that individuals can achieve more in more egalitarian societies. Others believe that high levels of personal achievement are possible only if individuals are free to succeed or fail according to their individual merits.
>
> What is your view of the relationship between equality and personal success?

Give reasons for your answer and include any relevant examples from your own knowledge or experience.

Write at least 250 words.

Additional model essays

Unit 1

The chart compares the percentage of male and female teachers in different educational settings from nursery school to university. Significant differences between men and women are evident.

Women held nearly all of the teaching posts in nursery and primary schools and the majority of posts in secondary schools (approximately 56%). They held the same percentage of posts as did men at college level. However, a smaller proportion of women held teaching positions at training institutes, and, at universities, female lecturers were outnumbered by males by roughly three to two.

For men, the pattern of employment was the reverse. Only 2% of nursery school teachers and 10% of primary teachers were men. They were more equally represented at secondary and college level. However, a significantly higher percentage of university lecturers were male (roughly 60%).

Overall, the figure shows that gender is a significant factor in patterns of employment within the education sector.

(151 words)

Bar charts are frequently used to compare information. Notice how the writer makes comparisons throughout.

The bar chart represents percentages not numbers. The words *percentage* and *proportion* are used throughout the response.

The writer makes reference to only four percentage figures out of a possible total of 12. This is enough to illustrate and support the main points. Remember, you do not need to include all of the information in the visual prompt.

The conclusion highlights the main point but does not offer an explanation. You are not required to explain or interpret the data.

The response meets the 150 word requirement but is not any longer than necessary. Remember, you should spend no more than 20 minutes on Task 1.

Unit 2

One of the most significant advances in civilisation is the development of modern methods of food production and preparation. Convenience foods have now become the norm in many societies. Although some people idealise traditional cooking practices and believe they will prevail indefinitely, demographic trends suggest that this is unlikely to be the case. In fact, there are a number of reasons for believing that convenience foods are likely to grow in popularity.

The first reason is the decline in family size and the increase in single-adult households. In more traditional societies, where families tended to be large, it made economic sense for one person to devote himself / herself to time-consuming domestic tasks such as growing and preparing food. Nowadays, people tend to live in ever smaller family units. If each family were to spend large amounts of time growing and processing food, this would be a poor use of society's human resource.

Another reason convenience foods are likely to become more popular is the increase in the number of adults, especially women with children, who work in full-time employment. In the UK, for example, working mothers significantly outnumber stay-at-home mothers. There is evidence that consumption of convenience foods rises with numbers of hours worked. As modern life increasingly demands that people are economically active, this trend is likely to continue.

Although many people still value traditional foods and methods of cooking, the trend towards smaller, dual-income households suggests that convenience foods are likely to continue to grow in popularity and may very well eventually replace traditional methods of food production and preparation.

(261 words)

This is a response to a type D 'Evaluate an idea' essay question. It asks the writer to consider the truth value of a prediction.

By acknowledging there is another point of view, the writer indicates that she has 'tested' her idea.

The writer structures her essay around reasons for her opinion. Notice how the word *reason* appears at the start of each body paragraph.

Examples to illustrate and support the argument are also given.

The response meets the 250-word requirement.

Unit 3

The bar chart shows the percentage of home and international students in the UK achieving at least a second class degree in eight subjects in 2018.

For the UK students, over half of the degrees awarded were second class or better. The largest percentage of good passes was in Art History and Sociology (80%) The lowest was in Information Technology (55%).

For international students, the rates were similarly high, though figures for individual subjects differed. In Electrical Engineering and Information Technology, four out of five degrees awarded to students from abroad were second class or better (versus fewer than two out of three for home students). However, the percentage gaining good degrees in subjects such as English Literature (55%) and Law (60%) was lower than the corresponding rate for home students (roughly 70%).

In brief, the chart shows that home students tended to do better in Arts and Social Science related subjects, whereas international students tended to do better in technology related subjects.

(163 words)

The simple present tense is used when referring to what the figure shows.

Quantities are referred to in a variety of ways.

The simple past tense is used here and in the remainder of the response because the data refers to 2018.

The writer uses superlatives when comparing more than two items, (in this case, eight subjects).

The writer uses comparatives when comparing two items, (in this case, international and home students).

The conclusion highlights the main idea but does not give reasons.

Unit 4

Unit 4 – Task 2

In recent years there has been growing awareness of the importance of preserving the world's biological diversity. As increasing numbers of unique, and potentially useful, plants and animals come under threat, people are beginning to ask whether more can be done to reverse this trend.

One possible approach is to regulate agricultural and industrial activity so that pollution and disruption to natural habitats is kept to a minimum. People argue that economic prosperity must be curtailed if it comes at the expense of the environment. However, businesses affected are unlikely to comply with such a strategy. It may even generate hostility to conservation efforts generally if the economic costs are perceived to be too high.

An alternative approach would be to protect and expand nature reserves so that complete ecosystems can be kept intact. This would ensure that a minimum number of wild plants and animals would survive. However, although such places are indeed valuable, experience shows that it is difficult to protect rare plants and animals from exploitation. In fact, as some species, like the tiger, become rarer, the more valuable they become to poachers and others who seek to benefit from their trade.

A more effective approach is to educate the public about the benefits of biodiversity. Money should be invested in the research and development of the world's biological resources. Once people understand that there are real benefits to exploiting natural resources in a sustainable way, they are more likely to make the short-term sacrifices necessary to preserve natural habitats.

(253 words)

This is a response to a type A 'Propose a solution to a problem' essay question.

This is a more academic way of saying *more and more*.

This is a less emotive and therefore more academic way of saying *are destroyed*.

The writer presents this idea impersonally by making *people* rather than I the subject of the sentence.

The writer begins with his least favoured option.

Notice that the writer does not use the contracted form *it's*.

The writer concludes with his preferred option. This makes the essay feel finished. Notice how the writer avoids using I and keeps his sentences short and simple.

Unit 5

Unit 5 – Task 1

The diagram gives information about the five principal writing systems used throughout the world: the Logographic, Adjad, Abjuda, Alphabetic, and Syllabic.

> The introduction indicates what the diagram shows.

Four of these are similar in that characters represent sounds. The oldest is the Abjad, used in Arabic, for example, where each character represents a consonant sound. Another is the Abjuda, used in the Indian Devanāgarī. Here, each character indicates a consonant plus vowel. The third system is the Alphabetic, used in English, for instance, where characters refer to a sound, either vowel or consonant. However, the relationship between pronunciation and spelling is sometimes approximate. Finally, in the Syllabic system, used in Japanese Kana for example, characters represent syllables.

> The superlative form is used because more than two items are compared.

> *Another* is used to signpost the second item in the list. Notice the remaining signposting expressions in this paragraph (*The third system* and *Finally*).

In addition to these four systems, there is also the Logographic system, which works on a different principle. Here, each character represents a word meaning. Therefore, languages which are different when spoken, such as Chinese and Japanese, can share written forms.

Overall, the diagram shows that most writing systems are based on sounds.

> The concluding sentence says something about the diagram as a whole. The word *overall* signals the conclusion.

(167 words)

Unit 6

Unit 6 – Task 2

The Internet has undoubtedly changed the way people shop. In some countries, buying and selling products online has become commonplace. Enthusiasts claim that the Internet offers consumers greater choice and flexibility. However, those who say that the Internet is transforming the lives of consumers are going too far.

Firstly, although online shopping appears to offer greater convenience, it is often rather risky and cumbersome in practice. Consumers cannot evaluate the quality of online products by handling them directly. Instead, they must rely on sellers to describe goods accurately in words and / or pictures. Mistakes can easily be made, leading to the inconvenience of having to exchange goods or seek a refund. Products bought online also normally need to be delivered by post. The convenience of online shopping thus hinges in part on the efficiency of the postal service.

Secondly, in spite of the promise of lower prices, Internet shopping seldom offers substantial savings. A competitive marketplace ensures that large price differentials rapidly disappear as suppliers align themselves with one another. Also, the cost of postage is normally borne by the buyer. A product that appears to be a bargain on screen often turns out to be no cheaper than the same product bought in a shop. Not surprisingly, only one in five purchases in the UK are made online.

For these reasons, Internet shopping is likely to remain a minority pursuit. The continuing popularity of shopping in the traditional way suggests that consumers continue to value its advantages: the opportunity to sample, compare and buy products in a real as opposed to a virtual space.

(265 words)

This is a response to a type D 'Evaluate an idea' essay question.

In this part of the introduction, the writer describes the context of the topic.

An opposing point of view is given using the emphatic reporting verb *claim*.

The writer expresses his point of view by challenging the opposing point of view.

This is the first generalisation, made less sweeping with the words *often* and *rather*.

This is the second generalisation, made less sweeping with the word *seldom*.

The writer gives his opinion (without using *I*).

The writer displays modesty by using the more tentative reporting verb *suggests*.

Unit 7

Figures 1 and 2 show economic growth and patterns of household expenditure from 2005 until 2020.

> The introduction briefly summarises what the figures show.

In 2005, economic growth was approximately 1%. The pie chart for that year shows that spending on essentials such as food and housing accounted for approximately two-thirds of total household expenditure. Spending on less essential items such as clothing, entertainment and travel was relatively modest at roughly 20%.

> This paragraph includes information from both figures. This pattern is repeated in the following paragraphs, which are sequenced chronologically.

Five years later, growth had roughly doubled and expenditure on essentials had shrunk as a proportion of total spending. Spending on non-essentials, in contrast, had expanded. This trend was even more marked in 2015, when growth peaked at approximately 4.5% and over 25% of expenditure was devoted to non-essentials.

> *In contrast* highlights difference.

> The comparative form (*more* + adjective) is used because two years are being compared.

However, the trend had reversed when in 2020 growth stood again at approximately 1% following an economic contraction. The pattern of expenditure in that year was similar to the pattern in 2005, though the contraction in non-essential spending was even more pronounced.

> The writer begins the paragraph with a generalisation.

Overall, the figures suggest that economic growth has an effect on patterns of household expenditure.

(169 words)

> The conclusion cautiously expresses a cause-and-effect relationship between figures 1 and 2 using the less emphatic reporting verb *suggest*.

Unit 8

No two families are alike. Therefore, the degree of control that it is appropriate for parents to exercise over their 14–15-year-old adolescent children is likely to vary from family to family. In this essay, I will outline three key variables that should be considered when attempting to make a decision about what is suitable in a given context.

One variable is the family's physical environment. Some environments clearly pose more dangers than others. Parents in an inner-city area with heavy traffic, a transient population and a high crime rate, for instance, probably need to supervise their children more closely than parents in a small rural community in which the residents know one-another.

Secondly, prevailing cultural norms are likely to be a factor. Some cultures, in Asia and the Middle East, for example, value social cohesion, whereas others, such as the US, tend towards individualism. One of the tasks of parents is to teach their children to function within their society; thus the degree of parental control will probably vary according to the type of society in which children are expected to take part.

The third, and perhaps most important consideration, is the personalities of the children involved. Children vary enormously in terms of traits such as maturity, impulsiveness, conscientiousness, and so on. The degree of parental control appropriate for one 14–15-year-old may not be at all appropriate for another.

In short, it is not possible to make recommendations regarding the supervision of adolescents that fit all contexts. The physical environment, the cultural context, and the personalities of those involved should all be considered.

(261 words)

This is a response to a type A 'Propose a solution to a problem' question.

The writer states her opinion.

Should is used to express a necessity.

The writer's intention is expressed using *will*.

Each body paragraph begins with a generalisation.

This is a supporting example, signalled with *for instance*.

This supporting example is signalled with *for example*.

These examples are signalled with *such as*.

may is used to make the statement less sweeping.

In short signals the conclusion.

The writer begins the conclusion by restating her opinion.

Here the writer summarises the main points.

Unit 9

The line graph shows three demographic trends in Scotland between 1940 and 2020: birth rate, population growth rate, and death rate.

> The colon is used to introduce a list.

Between 1940 and 1970, both birth rate and population growth rate fluctuated significantly. The birth rate started the period at 2.5% and ended at just over 1.0%. The population growth rate began and ended at approximately 1.0%, having peaked at 1.5% in 1955. The death rate, on the other hand, declined steadily until 1955 and then remained stable.

> The writer has organised this response chronologically, with all three trends compared in segments of time.

> *both ... and* links these trends.

Between 2000 and 2010, all three trends declined gradually. In about 1990, the death rate overtook the population growth rate for the first time; however, all three trends remained roughly static over the next ten years.

> *on the other hand* is a sentence linker signalling contrast. When placed after the subject of the sentence, it requires commas on either side.

Over the last decade, the birth rate and population growth rate have continued to decline, with the latter dipping below 0% in 2005. The death rate, in contrast, has risen slightly. This trend is projected to continue over the next ten years.

(157 words)

> *however* is a sentence linker. It is usually punctuated with a full stop or semicolon before, and a comma after.

> *with* can be used as a cohesive device.

> The writer uses the present perfect tense because the time frame is past to present.

> *This* + summary word (*trend*) ensures cohesion.

> This brief reference to the future is enough to make the passage feel complete. No separate conclusion is required.

> *the latter* is used to avoid repeating *population growth rate*.

Unit 10

Celebrities appear to play an increasingly prominent role in popular culture today. It is difficult to open a newspaper, switch on the television or browse the Internet without encountering an item of celebrity gossip. Not surprisingly, there are concerns about how this trend impacts on children, with some people claiming that children are being corrupted. This essay will argue that these fears are unnecessarily alarmist.

Firstly, some people maintain that children cannot distinguish between notoriety and genuine fame. However, in my experience, children usually admire footballers, singers and actors for their skill and achievements and express disappointment when they misbehave. Moreover, historically famous figures have also been flawed. In the past, many prominent political and business leaders had links with the slave trade, for example. Yet they are still presented to children as noteworthy individuals.

Another common fear is that children are being encouraged to pursue the unrealistic goal of achieving celebrity status themselves instead of working towards more socially useful occupations such as engineering, teaching or nursing. In fact, children have always had unrealistic fantasies about what they might do as adults, and these commonly reflect the preoccupations of their society. In the 19th century, for example, British children often aspired to being famous explorers. As children grow up, they learn to draw inspiration from their heroes and heroines without emulating them literally.

In short, there is little about today's celebrity culture that is fundamentally more harmful than the types of celebrity children have encountered in the past. Provided children are given appropriate guidance, they are unlikely to be adversely affected.

(262 words)

This is a response to a type D 'Evaluate an idea' question.

This adverb phrase shows the writer's attitude to the opinion expressed.

this + summary word (*trend*) links two sentences.

The writer states her intention using *will*. The subject of the sentence is *this essay* rather than *I*, in keeping with academic style.

The writer avoids repeating *celebrities* by listing common types of celebrities.

famous figures is used to avoid repetition.

prominent and *noteworthy* in the following sentence are synonyms for famous.

These are examples of socially useful occupations, signalled with *such as*.

commonly is a hedging expression, as is *often* in the following sentence.

Here, the conclusion begins with a summary of the main points.

Unit 11

Unit 11 – Task 1

The table compares four countries in terms the proportion of journeys undertaken by five modes of travel: car, bicycle, public transport, walking, and 'other'. The bar chart gives findings of a study into the reasons people in the USA drive.

Of the four countries compared, the USA was heavily reliant on cars, with only a small proportion of journeys made by other means (only 10% in total). The Netherlands, in contrast, showed a more even distribution of travel modes with fewer than half of all journeys made by car, a relatively large percentage made by bicycle (28%) and nearly one in five on foot. France and the UK fell between these two extremes.

The survey results shown in the bar chart may help explain why car use is higher in some countries than in others. The most cited reasons were the lack of alternative means of transport (38%) and the need to use a car for work (28%). However, convenience was also an important factor for over 20% of respondents.

(172 words)

Notice how the writer has paraphrased the task instructions.

with is used as a cohesive device in this and the following sentence.

Quantity is expressed in different ways. See also *one in five* in the following sentence.

When the task requires you to compare several figures, the information must be condensed.

The paragraph begins with a generalisation.

A superlative is used as a focussing expression for the supporting detail that follows.

The response does not end with a general summary. However, at 172 words it is sufficiently long. It also feels complete as the two figures are adequately linked and described.

Unit 12

Human beings have long struggled with the difficulty of ensuring both freedom and fairness in society. Some people argue that a good society is necessarily one that ensures equality for all. However, in my view, this is neither feasible nor desirable in practice.

| The writer makes reference to the opposing point of view to indicate that he has 'tested' his idea. |

Firstly, it is difficult to define universal standards of achievement. For some, achievement means material success, for others it may mean something else: a simple but altruistic life, for example. Bill Gates and Mother Teresa were very different but both achieved a great deal. Because people define achievement in different ways, it is difficult to determine what equality of opportunity might mean in practice.

| Each body paragraph begins with a generalisation. |

| *some* is used as a pronoun here to avoid repetition of *people* (see also *others* below). |

| This example supports the main point. |

Secondly, people differ in terms of their talents. Some people can make the most of scanty resources; others do very little with inherited wealth or educational opportunities. Many highly successful individuals have had little of either in their early years, yet achieved a great deal. The relationship between equality of opportunity and personal success is not straight forward.

| The writer signposts each key point. |

| Each body paragraph ends with a concluding sentence which refers back to the key word *equality*. This repetition ensures good cohesion. |

Finally, it is not easy to ensure a level playing field without damaging the incentive to do well. It is natural for parents to work hard in order to confer advantages on their children: private schooling, for example. It is difficult to see how equality of opportunity in education can be achieved without capping the aspirations of those who work hard.

| The writer maintains academic style by expressing his ideas impersonally. In this paragraph he uses a series of statements beginning *It is* + adjective. |

In short, while equality of opportunity is an attractive concept, attempting to put this ideal into practice can do more harm than good. People are different in terms of their values, talents and initiative. It is not possible to ensure equality without distorting what makes people unique.

| This sentence summarises the main idea. Notice how the opposing point of view is expressed in the subordinate clause and the writer's view is expressed in the main clause. This gives the writer's view greater weight. |

(273 words)

| The three main points of the body paragraphs are captured in the words *values, talents* and *initiative*. |

Answer key

Unit 1

Part 1: Language development
Adjectives and abstract nouns for describing character traits

Exercise 1

(Suggested answers)
Women d, e, g; Men a, b, c, f, h

Exercise 2
1 strengths
2 Gentleness
3 confidence
4 authority
5 compliance
6 Competition or Competitiveness

Exercise 3
1 c 2 c 3 a 4 f 5 d 6 a 7 e 8 b

Part 2: Exam skills
Task 1: Understanding the task

Exercise 1
1 20 minutes.
2 At least 150 words.
3 No, you should select and summarise the main features.
4 No.

Overview of task

Exercise 2
1 A statement about the type of information shown.
2 The fields which are dominated by men.
3 The fields which are dominated by women.
4 It makes a general statement about one of the main features of the chart.
5 They give supporting detail.
6 To provide a summary of the main message of the chart.

Task 2: Understanding the task

Exercise 3
1 a 2 b 3 a 4 a

Overview of task

Exercise 4
1 c 2 a 3 e 4 d 5 b

Exercise 5
1 Approximately 50 words.
2 Three.
3 Three.
4 From weakest solution to strongest solution.
5 To emphasise your opinion and summarise the main points.

Exercise 6
1 c: *Why do you think ...?*
2 d: *Do you think ... will ...?*
3 b: *To what extent should ...?*
4 a: *What can be done ...?*

Part 3: Exam practice

Task 1: Model answer

The bar chart gives information about male and female teachers in six types of educational institution in the UK in 2019. It shows what percentage of teachers were male and what percentage were female.

Women predominated in schools for children. This was particularly true of schools for very young children. Over 95 per cent of nursery school teachers, for example, were female. The situation was similarly one-sided in primary schools, where over 90 percent of teachers were women.

Men and women were more equally represented in teaching institutions catering for older children and young adults: secondary schools and colleges. College lecturers, for example, were 50 percent female and 50 percent male.

Males held a larger share of teaching posts in higher-level institutions. This was particularly true for universities, where male lecturers outnumbered female lecturers by a factor of three to two.

Overall, women were more likely to hold the more typically maternal role of teaching young children. Males, on the other hand, predominated in the higher status teaching role of university lecturer. Some people might say that there is no need to go further. However, in my view, wherever possible, gender equality should be encouraged.

[175 words]

Task 2: Model answer

There have always been differences in the types of work men and women have done. However, the trend in modern times has been for both men and women to have greater freedom of choice in terms of employment. Some people might say that there is no need to go further. However, in my view, wherever possible, gender equality should be encouraged.

There may indeed be good arguments for allowing certain posts to remain predominantly male or female. Where all-male or all-female groups exist, there may be a need for related posts to be held by men and women respectively. Patients in all-female hospital wards, for example, would

probably appreciate having female nurses to look after them. It could also be argued that certain jobs requiring a great deal of physical strength, coal mining or logging, for example, should continue to be done mainly by men.

However, in the vast majority of situations, making occupations more open to both genders has distinct advantages. Men and women can bring slightly different perspectives and approaches to a job. Female police officers, for example, may have a greater understanding of domestic violence and a better range of strategies for dealing with this problem. Male primary school teachers probably have a better understanding of the needs of young boys and can serve as good role models for them.

The changes that result from allowing men into female-dominated occupations and vice versa may be subtle, but they are far-reaching. However, to benefit the most from this development, it is important not to expect males and females to approach work in identical ways.

[266 words]

Exam tutor
1 You should write at least 150 words for Task 1 and at least 250 words for Task 2.
2 No, you should focus on summarising the key information and refer to enough detailed information to support your main points.
3 For your Task 2 essay you are expected to give your opinion about an issue; however, you should present your opinion in an objective fashion and use your general knowledge about the world rather than your personal experiences to support your main points.
4 You should spend more time writing your Task 2 essay.
5 Task 2 essay questions usually require you to do one of the following: propose one or more solutions to a problem, evaluate a solution to a problem, provide an explanation or prediction, evaluate an idea or belief.

Unit 2

Part 1: Language development

Expressions related to food and diet

Exercise 1
1 h 2 g 3 i 4 f 5 a 6 c 7 d 8 j 9 b 10 e

Exercise 2
1 i 2 g 3 h 4 b 5 c 6 a 7 d 8 e 9 f

Exercise 3
1 There was a moderate increase in the consumption of red meat.
2 There was then a rapid decline.
3 There was a steady rise in meat consumption.
4 There was a sharp fall again.
5 There was a gradual decrease in the annual consumption of red meat per person.

Time expressions related to line graphs

Exercise 4

Between 1918 and 1922, there was a moderate increase in the consumption of red meat from a low of 12 kgs to a high of 18 kgs per person. During the following ten-year period, it declined rapidly to its lowest point of just over 5 kgs. From 1950 to 1980, meat consumption rose steadily, reaching its highest point at 45 kgs. In 1980, It fell sharply again to approximately 30 kgs. From 1990 onwards, consumption of red meat per person decreased gradually by approximately 60 percent.

Exercise 5

(Model answer)

Between 1970 and 1990, consumption of fresh fruit and vegetables rose steadily from 100 grams to 300 grams per person per day. In the early to mid-1990s, it decreased to approximately 225 grams. There was then a further rise until 2005, when it reached a peak of 500 grams. Over the following ten years, consumption fluctuated between 400 and 500 grams per person. From 2010 to 2020, there was a steady fall in the consumption of fruit and vegetables to just over 300 grams. This trend is expected to continue until at least 2035.

Part 2: Exam skills

Task 1: Structuring a line graph response

Exercise 1
c

Exercise 2
b

Exercise 3

(Model answers)

Body paragraph 1: Overall food insecurity varied significantly. During the first four years, there was a gradual rise from 10% to 12%, followed by a fall to 10%. In 2008, there was a rapid increase to 18%. Levels remained high for six years; however, between 2014 and 2020, there was a gradual decrease to 12%.

Body paragraph 2: Over the twenty-year period, very low food security was experienced by between 2% and 6% of households. Between 2000 and 2006, the level fluctuated slightly. However, in 2006, two years before the rise in overall food insecurity, it increased sharply. After dipping slightly, levels of severe food insecurity remained relatively high at about 4% of households.

Task 2: Taking a stance on an issue

Exercise 4
Students' own answers.

Exercise 5
1 c, e, g
2 a, b, d, f

Generating ideas for your essay

Exercise 6
1 b 2 c 3 d 4 a 5 e 6 h 7 g 8 f

Exercise 7
Suggested answers
1 People who are too concerned with being slim could be considered vain.
2 It is healthier to be slim.
3 People who are overweight are more likely to suffer from health problems such as heart disease and diabetes.
4 Food labels can be complicated and misleading.
5 Most people are aware of the benefits of eating fresh food but still choose to eat fast foods instead.
6 People eat an unhealthy diet because they do not have time to buy and prepare fresh foods.
7 Modern life is busy with long working hours, long commutes to and from work, large choice of leisure activities.
8 Some of the healthiest foods are quick and easy to prepare, e.g. fresh fruit, salads.

Part 3: Exam practice

Task 1: Model answer

The graph shows the number of adolescents in the UK choosing a vegetarian diet between the years 1980 and 2020. Over the forty-year span, there were three periods of growth in the popularity of vegetarianism among young people.

in 1980, there were fewer than 200,000 vegetarian adolescents in the UK. Over the next five years, the number grew gradually to approximately 250,000, but by 1995 had declined again to 200,000. At that point, there was another significant rise in the number of adolescent vegetarians. By 2000, the numbers had reached a high of roughly 400,000, but then fell back before levelling off at about 300,000. The biggest rise occurred in 2015, when numbers of young vegetarians increased sharply. By 2020, there were over 900,000, nearly five times as many as in 1980.

Over this forty-year period, the number of adolescent vegetarians rose and fell every 10 to 15 years; however, the most remarkable increase occurred in the years 2015 to 2020 when the number more than trebled.

[167 words]

Task 2: Model answer

The increasing availability of convenience foods has been a significant feature of modern life in many developed countries. Some people have predicted that with advances in food technology, traditional foods and traditional methods of food preparation will disappear. In this essay, I will argue that this is unlikely to happen.

It is true that nowadays many people do not have enough time to cook and that convenience foods present an attractive option. These foods have improved significantly in terms of quality and availability, and the range of products for sale in the average supermarket is quite impressive. It is possible to find even very sophisticated ready-prepared meals suitable for the microwave oven.

However, the growing popularity of television and online cookery programmes, 'celebrity chefs', and glossy cookbooks suggest that people continue to value home cooking. Farmers markets selling fresh, locally-produced food continue to be the norm in many parts of the world. In fact, they are growing in popularity in countries such as the UK, where they had virtually disappeared from many towns and cities. This may be partly because cooking with natural ingredients is cheaper than buying processed foods.

Moreover, traditional foods are an important aspect of culture and social life. In many countries, traditional home-cooked meals continue to be shared in regular family gatherings. Important celebrations such as weddings, Christmas, and Chinese New Year are marked by traditionally prepared feasts.

In spite of the utility of convenience foods, people are unlikely to abandon practices that are economically sound and give them great pleasure. It is hard to imagine a world in which people do not continue to enjoy traditional home-cooked meals.

[273 words]

1 verb + adverb (e.g. *xxxx increased rapidly*) and *there + to be* + adjective + noun (*+ -ing*) (e.g. *There was a rapid increase in xxx*).
2 Information about the time frame (e.g. *between 1950 and 2000*) and specific figures from the graph (e.g. *from 200 grams to 300 grams*)
3 A Task 1 response typically begins with statements about the kind of information shown in the visual prompt and ends with a brief summary of the most significant information or message from the prompt.
4 Yes, this allows you to show that you have 'tested' your opinion by comparing it with another opinion.
5 Yes, if you acknowledge that your opinion is not perfect you can show that you are fair-minded.

Unit 3

Part 1: Language development

College and university subjects

Exercise 1
Arts and Humanities: philosophy, media studies, English literature, history
Social Sciences: business studies, sociology, law, psychology
Science and Technology: mathematics, chemistry, biology, engineering

Collocations related to education

Exercise 2
1 e   2 f   3 b   4 a, c, g   5 d, e   6 b, g   7 a

Exercise 3
1 rote learning   2 critical thinking   3 formal examinations
4 higher education   5 continuous assessment   6 educational standards

Expressing quantity

Exercise 4
1 c   2 a   3 f   4 b   5 d   6 e

Exercise 5
1 A small minority   2 The vast majority   3 Just under a third
4 Nearly half   5 Roughly one in four   6 Three quarters

Part 2: Exam skills

Task 1: Comparing and contrasting information

Exercise 1
1 b   2 e   3 a   4 d   5 f   6 c

Exercise 2
1 as … as   2 lower   3 least   4 fewer   5 higher   6 lowest

Describing information in bar charts

Exercise 3
1 D: *On the other hand*   2 D: *Whereas*   3 S: *similar*
4 S: *both*

Exercise 4
1 Fewer male candidates than female candidates passed their English examinations.
2 As many males as females achieved a passing grade in mathematics.
3 Whereas men did well in technology-related subjects, women did well in language-related subjects.
4 The number of passes in religious studies was lower for male candidates than for female candidates.
5 Similar numbers of male and female students passed the economics exam.

Task 2: Selecting and organising ideas

Exercise 5
1 She is against the idea that formal written examinations can measure intelligence.
2 The writer has omitted: 'Exams can be designed to include a variety of tasks to measure different kinds of intelligence' and 'Other methods of measuring intelligence could be less fair and systematic'.
3 The writer wants to present more points to support her position and fewer points in favour of the other position.
4 The writer presents her preferred position last so that she can make a strong conclusion.

Writing an essay outline

Exercise 6

(Suggested answers)

What are the possible solutions?	Positive consequence(s)	Drawback(s)
Solution in the question: Cram schools	Cram schools can support students' learning It is reasonable to seek opportunities to practise skills that are difficult, e.g. taking exams	Attending cram schools can be stressful Cram schools are unfair because they give advantage to students who can afford to pay
Other possible solution: We should ensure schools are good enough for all students	Discouraging parents from sending their children to cram schools would improve pupils' well being If students and teachers work hard in schools, there is no need for additional cramming	There will always be differences in the quality of schools There will always be businesses that exploit people's fears about not being good enough

Exercise 7

(Example essay plan)

Introduction:	cram schools are big business, but they may not be a good thing
Body paragraph 1:	**solution in the question:** Cram schools serve a need
	points for: • Many students who attend such schools do well in exams • Cram schools can support students' learning
	points against: • Cram schools teach students to be 'test wise' rather than to learn • Attending cram schools can be stressful • Cram schools are unfair because they give advantage to students who can afford to pay
Body paragraph 2:	**other possible solution:** ensure schools are good enough for all students
	points against: • There will always be businesses that exploit people's fears about not being good enough
	points for: • Discouraging parents from sending their children to cram schools would improve pupils' well being • If students and teachers work hard in schools, there is no need for additional cramming • In countries with exams that properly reflect the curriculum, there are few cram schools
Conclusion:	cram schools are a symptom of a faulty educational system

Part 3: Exam practice

Task 1: Model answer

The bar chart shows the proportion of UK students and international students achieving second class degrees or higher in seven different subjects at a university in the UK.

Degree results were generally good for both home and international students, with well over 50 percent gaining a second-class degree or better in all seven subjects except International Law. International students tended to do better than UK students in technology-related subjects. This was particularly true of Information Technology. Whereas over 80 percent of international students gained a good degree in IT, only about half of the UK students did so.

Degree results were similar for the two groups in Nursing and Accounting. In Arts and Social Science-related subjects, UK students tended to do better. The biggest gap in performance was in International Law, where three-quarters of UK students gained a second-class degree or better. In contrast, fewer than half of the international students attained this level.

Overall, the chart suggests that international and UK students had different strengths when studying for degrees in this UK university.

[174 words]

Task 2: Model answer

Examinations are one of the most common methods of measuring learning in education systems throughout the world. At virtually every stage of the learning process, exams

are used to verify that the learner is ready to move on to the next stage. However, many people believe that the role of examinations should be reconsidered.

There are clearly certain advantages to exams. They help to ensure fairness by imposing the same conditions on all exam candidates. They are also relatively versatile; different types of exam questions, for example, multiple-choice questions and essay tasks, can test different sorts of reasoning ability.

However, exams also have clear drawbacks. Test-wise candidates can often perform well on exams without having good underlying knowledge or skills. On the other hand, some test-takers perform poorly in exams simply because of anxiety. Some teachers and learners focus only on those aspects of the curriculum that are likely to be tested, thus narrowing the educational experience for all.

A number of measures should be taken to address these concerns. Wherever possible, exams should match the content and activities of the learning environment. Exam tasks should be varied to give fair opportunities to candidates with different types of skills. Other types of assessment should also be considered; assignment writing, for example, to assess independent learning and research skills, or group projects, to measure teamwork ability.

Exams clearly have a role to play in ensuring proper, objective assessment of achievement. However, exams need to be carefully designed and supplemented with other forms of assessment if they are to be a truly useful component of the educational system.

[266 words]

Exam tutor

1 No, you should categorise and compare the information.
2 Use comparative forms when comparing two items; use superlative forms when comparing one item with the remainder of the group.
3 No, you should use expressions such as *nearly half, almost two-thirds, the vast majority*. Words can often convey the information in a more meaningful way and allow you show your language skills.
4 Having a plan in mind before you write and essay allows you to write more quickly and focus on effective and accurate expression.
5 Comparing different ideas in an essay can allow you to demonstrate a wide range of language skills.

Unit 4

Part 1: Language development
Nature and environment expressions

Exercise 1
1 b 2 a 3 e 4 f 5 d 6 c

Exercise 2
1 Intensive farming 2 Acid rain 3 logging 4 Overgrazing
5 oil spills 6 global warming 7 Strip mining

Expressions to describe cause and effect

Exercise 3
1 has led to, causes, has contributed to, result in, has been
  attributed to

2 is associated with, is linked to
3 *Contribute to* implies there is more than one cause.

Exercise 4
1 b 2 c 3 e 4 a 5 d

Exercise 5
1 Intensive farming has contributed to a significant decline in
  biodiversity.
2 Vegetation has been lost; consequently, the insect
  population has declined.
3 There are fewer insects, so the small animals that feed on
  them have moved elsewhere.
4 There have been fewer predators, such as owls, because of
  the disappearance of prey species.

Part 2: Exam skills
Task 1: Describing a process

Exercise 1
a pioneer plants b gather moisture c return organic material to the soil d shrubs

Exercise 2
a If the process is natural, you normally use the active voice.
b If there is a human agent, you normally use the passive voice.

Clear cutting

The flow chart <u>illustrates</u> the process of clear cutting, a logging practice which <u>involves</u> the complete removal of trees from a given area.

Firstly, access roads to the area <u>are cut</u>. Secondly, the entire crop of standing trees <u>is felled</u> by mechanized harvesters. The trees <u>are</u> then <u>extracted</u>, and <u>brought</u> to the road side.

Once the trees <u>have been extracted</u>, they <u>are processed</u> by chain saw. The limbs and tree tops <u>are removed</u>. The stems <u>are 'bucked'</u>, that <u>is, cut</u> into logs of a specified length. The logs <u>are</u> then <u>sorted</u> by size and <u>loaded</u> onto logging trucks for transport to the sawmill.

In the final stage of clear cutting, the land <u>is prepared</u> for future harvests. The remaining scrub <u>is gathered</u> into large piles and <u>burnt</u>.

Forest regrowth

Following a period of widespread deforestation, forest regrowth <u>occurs</u> over a series of phases.

The first plants <u>to grow</u> <u>are</u> 'pioneer' plants, which <u>can</u> <u>survive</u> in harsh conditions. They <u>provide</u> shade, <u>gather</u> moisture, and <u>return</u> organic material to the soil. In <u>doing</u> so, they <u>create</u> the conditions for other plants <u>to thrive</u>.

In the second phase of regrowth, shrubs <u>emerge</u>. They quickly <u>cover</u> the ground, <u>crowding</u> out the pioneers. However, they too eventually <u>die</u> off as young trees <u>push</u> through the brush. Within ten years, trees finally <u>take</u> over, <u>preventing</u> light from <u>reaching</u> the forest floor.

Combining sentences in a process description

Exercise 3

1 The first plants to grow are pioneer plants, which can survive in harsh conditions.
2 They provide shade, gather moisture and return organic material to the soil.
3 They quickly cover the ground, crowding out the pioneers.
4 However, they too eventually die off as young trees push through the brush.
5 The logs are then sorted by size and loaded onto logging trucks for transport to the sawmill.
6 Once the trees have been extracted, they are processed by chainsaw.

Exercise 4

(Model answer)

> The maps show changes that have taken place on the island between 1970 and 2019.
>
> Over the fifty-year period, large areas of native forest in the north-east and the south were removed and partially replaced with palm oil plantations. The area of intact forest in the west shrank as roads were built and logging increased. Dams were constructed in the east, flooding the area and further reducing the extent of native forest.

Task 2: Writing in an academic style

Exercise 5

1 Response 1 is informal in style; Response 2 is academic in style.
2 Response 2 is more impersonal and less emotional. There are no colloquialisms or contracted forms.

Response 1

In my opinion, it's true that humans and animals sometimes have conflicting interests. Everybody exploits animals for food and clothing, and farmers have used more and more wild land for farming. But should we keep on doing this?

In parts of the world where the population is growing, and there isn't enough food to go around, the conflict between humans and animals is really awful. For example, if you go to Africa, you can see large nature reserves next to really poor human settlements. I love the idea of elephants and lions living in the wild. But it's often the poor farmer living nearby who loses out.

Response 2

It may be true that humans and animals sometimes have conflicting interests. Most people exploit animals for food and clothing, and farmers have brought ever increasing areas of wild land into cultivation. However, whether this process should continue is a question that needs careful consideration.

In parts of the world where the population is growing and resources are scarce, the conflict between humans and animals is particularly problematic. This can be seen in parts of Africa, for example, where large nature reserves lie next to very poor human settlements. People living thousands of miles away may value the idea of elephants and lions living in the wild. However, it is often the poor farmer living nearby who is denied access to land and potential earnings.

Exercise 6

Characteristics of academic style	Examples from Responses 1 and 2	
	Informal style	Academic style
Academic style tends to be less personal. Avoid: • overusing personal pronouns and adjectives (e.g. *I, you, my, your*) • addressing the reader directly	*In my opinion, it's true* *should we keep on doing this?* *if you go to Africa, you can see I*	*It may be true* *whether…careful consideration* *This can be seen in parts of Africa* *People living thousands of miles away*
Academic style tends to be less emotional. Avoid: • exaggeration (e.g. *totally, perfect*) • emotive words (e.g. *terrible, adore*) • words that express value judgments (e.g. *immoral*)	*Everybody exploits* *awful* *love*	*Most people exploit* *problematic* *may value*
Academic style normally requires: • fewer conjunctions (e.g. *and, but*) • more subordinators (e.g. *whereas, because*) • more sentence linkers (e.g. *nevertheless, therefore*)	*But*	*However,*
Academic style is more formal. Avoid: • contracted forms (e.g. *isn't, he's*) • the words *get, a lot of* and *really* • double comparatives (e.g. *more and more*) • phrasal verbs (e.g. *take up, break out*) • colloquial expressions or sayings (e.g. *every coin has two sides*)	*it's* *really* *more and more* *there isn't enough food to go around* *loses out*	*it is* *particularly / very* *ever increasing* *resources are scarce* *is denied access to land and potential earnings*

Exercise 7

(Model answer)

However, in relation to plants, the advantages of conservation are more apparent. Wild plants are not just beautiful; they are also a very valuable resource. Throughout history, people have used wild plants to make medicines such as aspirin for example. Also, if certain varieties of crops are prone to disease, wild plants could be used to develop new varieties. Because there are many plants that have not yet been discovered, their potential uses remain unknown.

To sum up, it is worth trying to preserve natural habitats because wild animals and plants are unique and could save lives. However, it is important to remember that people's basic needs are also important. Therefore, the burden of protecting plant and animal species should be distributed fairly.

Exercise 8

(Suggested answer)

1 It could be argued that the desire for wealth encourages people to exploit the environment.
2 Environmental degradation may be unavoidable because there is no way of enforcing international agreements. Leaders may sign such agreements simply to create a favourable impression in the media.

Part 3: Exam practice

Task 1: Model answer

The flow chart shows what typically occurs as a consequence of deforestation. When trees are removed, there are four main immediate effects, which eventually result in flooding, degraded vegetation and a loss of biodiversity.

One immediate effect is soil which has been compacted by heavy equipment. The resulting hard, 'baked' soil contributes to the run off of rain water and, eventually, flooding.

Another immediate consequence of logging is a reduction in the number of roots holding the soil together. This leads to soil erosion. As a consequence, the quality and variety of vegetation is compromised.

The third immediate effect is burning, both deliberate and as a consequence of an increased risk of forest fires. The waste that remains after logging is destroyed and the microorganisms that feed on this material are lost. This leads to degraded vegetation.

The final immediate consequence is a reduction in the amount of moisture plants return to the air. Because there is less moisture in the air, there is less precipitation and an increased incidence of drought. This too reduces plant growth and ultimately results in degraded vegetation and a loss of biodiversity.

[188 words]

Task 2: Model answer

As natural resources come under increasing pressure, the list of endangered plants and animals continues to grow. The causes are many: developments in agriculture, mining, forestry and transport. Some would argue that the loss of biodiversity is a price we must pay for progress. In my view, however, there is much that governments can and should do to protect the world's plants and animals.

Governments could promote greater understanding of plants and animals by investing in the research and preservation efforts of universities, zoos, and botanical institutes. This may ensure the survival of individual species and produce tangible benefits in the form of new medicines and products. However, this strategy alone would do little to protect whole ecosystems that are under threat.

An alternative strategy would be to protect natural habitats by expanding nature reserves. This would have immediate positive consequences for those areas by preserving delicate ecosystems. However, this strategy also has limitations. It does not protect from phenomena such as acid rain and water pollution, which can cross boundaries and affect large areas.

The most effective solution is to limit the damage at its source. Companies that engage in practices that harm the environment should be required to demonstrate that they have taken all reasonable efforts to minimise the damage. Public contracts for roads and buildings should only be awarded to firms that have a good environmental track record.

The strategies outlined above: preservation, protection and, above all, prevention, can do much to reverse the destruction that threatens the world's plants and animals. The aesthetic and practical benefits of doing so are well worth the cost.

[268 words]

Exam tutor

1 To suggest a possible cause and effect relationship, use phrases such as *is linked to* or *is associated with*.
2 Use the passive voice when the subject of the action is unknown or less important than the action itself.
3 The active voice is commonly used to describe natural processes; the passive voice is often used to describe man made processes.
4 For a less emotional style, avoid using exaggeration
   (e.g. *totally, perfect*), emotive words (e.g. *terrible, adore*), and words that express strong value judgements (e.g. *immoral*).
5 For a formal style, avoid contracted forms (e.g. *isn't, he's*), the words *get, a lot of* and *really*, double comparatives (e.g. *more and more*), phrasal verbs (e.g. *take up, break out*), colloquial expressions or sayings (e.g. *every coin has two sides*).

Unit 5

Part 1: Language development

Expressions associated with languages

Exercise 1
1 mother tongue   2 official language   3 second language
4 lingua franca   5 non-native   6 bilingual   7 standard form
8 minority languages

Reporting verbs for different functions

Exercise 2
1 maintain, claim   2 admit, concede   3 deny, challenge, object to   4 urge

Emphatic, neutral and tentative reporting

Exercise 3
1 argue   2 question   3 doubt   4 accept   5 suggest
6 suspect   7 doubt

Exercise 4
1 c   2 a   3 d   4 b

Part 2: Exam skills

Task 1: Creating a coherent structure

Exercise 1
Order: c, d, a, b

Exercise 2
1 Paragraphs a and d make generalisations about the whole diagram. Paragraphs b and c give specific information about parts of the diagram.
2 The introduction identifies the type of information shown by the diagram; the conclusion makes a general statement about the information.
3 General to specific.

Exercise 3
1 b
2 c
3 It repeats the words in the task instructions.
4 It has too much detailed information.

Introductions and conclusions

Exercise 4

(Suggested answers)

1 The bar chart shows the proportion of children in European secondary schools who are studying five different foreign languages in the years 2000, 2010 and 2020.

3 In summary, the figure shows that some of the more dominant world languages, English in particular, are being more widely taught, whereas other languages, with the exception of Spanish, are becoming less popular.

Task 2: Developing an introduction

Exercise 5
1 c / b   2 b   3 d   4 e

Exercise 6
1 It begins with the context and ends with the writer's opinion.
2 The last position makes the sentence more prominent.

Presenting your view effectively

Exercise 7
1 e   2 e   3 b   4 g   5 d

Exercise 8
Order: 3, 5, 2, 1, 4

Exercise 9
1 the world becomes   2 increasingly important   3 therefore
4 right approach   5 I will outline   6 the most effective methods

Exercise 10

(Model answer)

As anyone who has travelled abroad will know, misunderstandings can easily occur among people from different cultures. It is sometimes assumed that this happens because the people involved do not have an adequate knowledge of the language. However, I would argue that more than language knowledge is required to communicate successfully. This essay will examine what I believe to be the most important factors in communication breakdown.

Part 3: Exam practice

Task 1: Model answer

The diagram shows the languages of Europe, Iran, and the Indian subcontinent and how they are related through a common Indo-European root language.

There are seven main branches: three represent the languages spoken throughout Western Europe, and four represent the languages spoken further to the east. The Western European branches include the Celtic, Germanic, and Italic languages. Some of these languages, such as Gaelic or Welsh, are spoken by relatively few people, but others, including German and English (from the Germanic branch) and French and Spanish (Italic branch) are among the most widely spoken languages in the world.

The eastern Indo-European branches include the languages spoken in Iran, the Indian Subcontinent, Greece, and the Slavic countries. The Indian branch comprises several languages including Hindi, Urdu and Bengali. The Slavic branch covers languages spoken in Eastern Europe, such as Russian and Polish, as well as Czech.

Overall, the diagram shows that languages that are commonly regarded as very different are, in fact, related.

[162 words]

Task 2: Model answer

As the world becomes more integrated, the need for common means of communication is becoming more pressing. Inevitably, speakers of minority languages have been under pressure to speak the languages of more dominant groups, both locally and globally. Some people argue that there is nothing that can or should be done to stop this process. I would suggest that the issue merits more careful consideration.

It is true that as the balance of power among groups of people throughout history has shifted, languages have arisen, changed, and died out. Even once widely-spoken languages, such as Latin, have disappeared. To some extent, therefore, this process may be inevitable. However, there are examples of communities that have managed to preserve and even revive languages under threat. Irish and Scots Gaelic, for example, have been preserved by government policy on education and broadcast media.

There are, indeed, several benefits to preserving minority languages. Retaining the language of a community often means that other forms of culture are maintained: songs, literature and local traditions. These all contribute to the richness and variety of human culture. Moreover, language helps communities to remain cohesive and to have a strong sense of identity. This can help people to be strong in adversity. Where this sense of identity and cohesion has been lost, for example among many indigenous communities in North America, problems can follow: low self-esteem, lack of confidence and loss of initiative.

In short, it is possible and, in many cases, desirable, to make the effort to preserve minority languages. This can have benefits both for the minority speech community and for society as a whole in terms of cultural richness.

[275 words]

Exam tutor

1 To express agreement: *agree, accept, acknowledge, support, admit, concede*
   To express disagreement: *disagree, doubt, question, dismiss, refute, deny, challenge*
2 You should use mainly your own words.
3 State the topic of the essay; write something about the general context; explain why the topic is interesting, relevant or important; present a viewpoint that you will challenge; present your own viewpoint; state the purpose of the essay; outline the structure of the essay.
4 It is generally more effective to express your opinion towards the end of your introduction.

Unit 6

Part 1: Language development

Technology expressions

Exercise 1

1 c 2 e 3 d 4 b 5 a 6 f

Adjectives for highlighting key points

Exercise 2

1 f 2 c 3 d 4 b 5 e 6 a

Exercise 3

1 noticeable 2 distinctive 3 underlying 4 main
5 widespread

Language for moderating statements

Exercise 4

Quantifiers: many, most
Verbs: tend, appear
Modal verbs: might, may
Adverbs of frequency: rarely, often
Adverbs of probability: probably

Exercise 5

(Suggested answers)

1 Some people over the age of sixty have difficulty grasping new technology.
2 Excessive use of social media can sometimes cause mental health problems.
3 Online shopping is possibly addictive.
4 Too much screen time may make some children less active.
5 It is possible that some of the world's problems could be solved by advances in science and technology.

Part 2: Exam skills

Task 1: Interpreting information presented in tables

Exercise 1

1 Response 2 is more satisfactory. In Response 1, the writer has simply reproduced the information in the table in words. The response is also somewhat short (138 words). In Response 2, the writer has highlighted the significant aspects of the data by emphasizing main points and supporting these with detailed information from the table.
2 In both responses, the first and last sentences contain main points (*The table shows that … Overall …*). In Response 2, the first line of body paragraph 1 (*One of the most significant changes was …*) and of body paragraph 2 (*Another noticeable trend was …*) also contain general statements.
3 In Response 1, there is a general point in the introduction and a general point in the conclusion; all of the detailed information is contained in the middle body paragraph. In Response 2, there are four general statements, one at the start of each paragraph. The general statements in the body paragraphs are followed by detailed information.

Exercise 2

1 There has been significant growth in Internet use worldwide; Internet users now make up 57 percent of the population. The most significant figure is probably the percentage change (1,115 percent).
2 The most obvious groupings are probably the technologically advanced regions (Europe, North America and Australia / Oceania) and the developing regions (Asia, Africa, Latin America and the Middle East).
3 The more developed regions have the highest percentages of Internet users – all 80 percent or higher. The developing regions have lower percentages – between 36 and 67 percent.
4 The developing regions have all experienced the highest rates of growth in Internet users. The developed regions have experienced the lowest rates of growth.

Exercise 3

(Suggested answers)

1 One significant trend is the high percentage of Internet users in the most economically developed regions of the world. Eighty-nine percent of the population of North America, for example, use the Internet. Europeans are the next in rank at eighty-eight percent, followed by Australia and Oceania at eighty percent.
2 The smallest growth in the percentage of Internet users occurred in the most developed regions of the world. Growth in North America, which has the highest percentage of Internet users, was the lowest at 200 percent. Australia and Europe also experienced relatively low percentage increases in Internet users at 275 and 585 percent respectively.

3 Another noticeable feature of the information in the table is the relatively low percentage of Internet users in the least developed regions of the world. Less than seventy percent of the populations of Africa, Asia, the Middle East, and Latin America use the Internet. The region with the smallest percentage of Internet users was Africa at thirty-six percent.

4 However, the biggest growth in Internet users occurred in developing regions. The percentage of the population online in Africa, for instance, grew more than a hundred-fold. The Middle East, Latin America, and Asia also saw Internet use grow significantly There were fifty times more Internet users in the Middle East in 2018 than there were in 2008, and nearly twenty times more people online in Asia over the same period.

Task 2: Planning an essay

Exercise 4
Strengths: It has a clear structure. There are good supporting points for each of the two general statements.
Weaknesses: The essay does not seem to have a fully developed discussion because the points for and against are listed separately. The introduction contains a cliché (a double-edged sword).

Exercise 5

(Model answer)

People who live in countries with developed economies often take access to information technology for granted. They find it hard to imagine a world in which this technology does not bring greater prosperity for everyone. However, as the IT revolution moves forward, some people are left behind. Indeed, there are several barriers to wider IT access and its potential benefits.

One major barrier is inadequate infrastructure. In some areas, fast broadband speeds may only be available in major cities, putting many rural areas off the map as far as IT access is concerned. In these circumstances, the Internet may actually be increasing rather than decreasing social inequality between urban and rural areas. A lack of reliable access to the Internet not only disadvantages rural populations but also rural businesses, which may not be able to sell their goods online.

Poverty is another major factor when it comes to the digital divide. People on low incomes cannot always afford electronic devices or broadband. They may even struggle to pay for electricity at times. Internet access for them may be a luxury.

Illiteracy also remains an obstacle to IT access, even in developed nations. In some areas, many adults struggle to read. Older women and the poor are at greater risk of having poor literacy and are therefore at a disadvantage when it comes to IT access and its potential benefits.

In short, where unequal access to infrastructure, wealth, and education exists, the IT revolution is unlikely to reduce inequality. Unless fundamental inequalities are addressed, the Internet may, in fact, increase social divides.

Body paragraph 1, Evidence for positive effect: e
Body paragraph 2, Evidence for a positive effect: d, f
Body paragraph 3, Evidence for negative effect: c
Body paragraph 3, Evidence for negative effect: g
The advantage of this plan is that it has a more sophisticated structure. Points for and against are arranged thematically, rather than simply listed. This allows you to contrast the evidence for and against using complex sentences, e.g. *Although* …

Developing a paragraph

Exercise 6
1 basic infrastructure is not universally good (G)
   broadband access lacking, especially in rural areas (S)
   people and business affected by slow broadband (S)
2 poverty is one aspect of the problem (G)
   people on low income cannot afford broadband (S)
   the poor even struggle to pay for electricity (S)
3 lack of literacy skills is an obstacle (G)
   in some areas, many adults have poor literacy (S) older women and the poor more likely to have lower levels of literacy (S)

Part 3: Exam practice

Task 1: Model answer

The table shows the average length of online video advertisements by sector and the average length of time viewers spent watching these advertisements.

The average length of the advertisements varied from a low of 14.6 seconds for clothing to a high of 45.8 for public service advertisements. With the exception of government- and entertainment-related advertisements, in general, products and services which required a large financial commitment tended to have longer advertisements. Cars, financial services and travel advertisements, for example, were all eighteen seconds on average or longer. Less expensive products, on the other hand, such as consumer electronics, clothing and medicines, tended to have shorter advertisements.

Adverts for more expensive products or services also tended to be watched for longer than adverts for less expensive items. Viewers on average watched more than 50 percent of advertisements for cars, financial services and travel. In contrast, viewers tended to watch less of government advertisements and advertisements for cheaper goods such as consumer electronics, clothing and medicines.

Overall, length of online video advertisements and length of time spent viewing such advertisements appears to be associated with the perceived cost of the product or service being advertised.

[194 words]

Task 2: Model answer

New technologies, in particular, the Internet, are undoubtedly having a major impact on the way goods and services are bought and sold. In many countries, buying products online has become a mainstream activity.

Now in the UK, for example, nearly twenty per cent of all retail trade is conducted online. While some people argue that the actual impact of the Internet on shopping is overstated, I would argue that it is in fact quite significant for two main reasons.

The first reason is that the development of online shopping has meant that the market for goods available to the individual has grown exponentially. It is possible to buy almost anything in the world-wide online retail market: exotic foods, art works, rare books, adventure holidays. Products that were once only available to people who lived in large cosmopolitan cities can now be bought by people living in small towns and remote areas.

Another significant reason is that the buyer can have more control over the process. Price comparison websites make it easier to find bargains. Shopping can be done at any time of the day or night, and shoppers can browse for as long as they like without pressure from sales assistants. This means that shoppers can potentially become more knowledgeable about the products they are buying. Because of the greater competition involved in trading within a large market, sellers are under pressure to improve the quality of their products.

In short, online shopping has shifted the balance of power in favour of the consumer. Consumers not only have wider access to goods but also have greater access to information and more control over how they shop. The unfortunate side effect is the closure of many traditional shops and the resulting negative impact on the people they employ.

[297 words]

Exam tutor

1 *distinctive, main, noticeable, significant, underlying, widespread.*
2 Task 2, because you cannot directly reference supporting evidence for your claims.
3 Begin by highlighting a significant aspect of the data, then support your main point with detailed information from the visual prompt.
4 No, you should include enough detail to exemplify and support your main points.
5 If you arrange points thematically, you can show more skill in argumentation. Rather than simply listing points for and against, you can contrast evidence for and against using complex sentences.

Unit 7

Part 1: Language development
Personal finances and spending expressions

Exercise 1
1 housing   2 transportation   3 entertainment   4 food
and drink   5 dining out   6 clothing and footwear   7 home
furnishings   8 utilities

Exercise 2
1 Disposable income   2 personal debt   3 goods and services
4 consumer confidence   5 Household expenditure

Exercise 3
1 financial   2 saved   3 costly   4 on credit   5 criteria
6 quantity   7 behaviour

Using precise language
Exercise 4
1 products   2 aspects of   3 take action   4 advantages
5 their necessities   6 their possessions

Part 2: Exam skills
Task 1: Describing the relationship between two visual prompts

Exercise 1
1 Both figures relate to consumer spending.
2 It is reasonable to assume a cause and effect relationship.
3 If you look at the overall trends, you may notice a
   connection between the disposable income of the
   three age groups and the sales figures for the products
   likely to be purchased by people in these age groups.
   Any obvious points, for example peaks and low points
   that help to illustrate the connection, should be
   highlighted.
4 You can highlight the connections most effectively by
   comparing features of both figures in each paragraph.

Exercise 2
1 The first sentence gives a description of what is shown in
   Figure 1; the second sentence gives a description of what
   is shown in Figure 2; the third sentence makes a statement
   about the relationship between Figures 1 and 2.
2 Cause and effect: *Seen together, the figures suggest a link
   between …*
3 In paragraph 1, the writer describes the overall trend in
   disposable income for 15–24 year-olds, then the overall
   trend in sales for the products most likely to be purchased
   by that age group.
   In paragraph 2, the writer describes the overall trend in
   disposable income for 35–44 year-olds, then the overall
   trend in sales for the products most likely to be purchased
   by that age group.
   In paragraph 3, the writer describes the overall trend in
   disposable income for 65–74 year-olds, then the overall
   trend in sales for the products most likely to be purchased
   by that age group.
4 The writer focuses on the most notable feature of both
   trends because this is sufficient to demonstrate that there is
   a connection.
5 *showed a similar pattern; also; not surprisingly … also*
6 *may be influenced by*

Expressing cause and effect relationships tentatively

Exercise 3

Suggested answers
Alternatives for Sentence 1:
When the availability of cheap credit rises, levels of consumer
spending also appear to rise.
The more cheap credit is available, the more consumers spend.

Alternatives for Sentence 2:
When the rate of taxation falls, levels of consumer spending
appear to rise.
The less consumers are taxed, the more they spend.

Exercise 4

Suggested answer

Figure 1 shows the percentage change in the amount of credit available and taxation between 1990 and 2020. The second figure shows the percentage increase in expenditure on three different types of products at five-year intervals between 2000 and 2020.

Seen together, the two figures suggest that there is a positive correlation between the availability of credit and levels of consumer spending. The amount of credit available reached a peak in 2005, when nearly 60% more credit was available than in 1990, and another high point in 2020. Spending on all three categories of expenditure (food, entertainment and clothing) also reached high points at approximately the same time.

On the other hand, the level of consumer spending appears to be inversely proportional to the rate of taxation. When taxation fell sharply in the periods leading up to 2005, consumer spending appeared to increase sharply. The similar pattern is evident in the period between 2008 and 2020.

Overall, greater availability of credit appears to act as a stimulus to consumer spending, whereas higher taxation may have the opposite effect.

Task 2: Signposting examples and supporting evidence

Exercise 5

1 Response 2 is more satisfactory because it contains examples to illustrate and support the main point. Response 1 essentially repeats the main point in three different ways.
2 States the main point
3 Sentence 2 further explains the main point, sentence 3 gives an example to illustrate the main point, sentence 4 supports the main point.
4 *This can be seen, for example, when …*
5 *Indeed*

Exercise 6

1 *for example* or *for instance*
2 *An example of this*
3 *indeed* or *in fact*

Developing a paragraph with examples and evidence

Exercise 7
(Suggested answers)

> **1** Some people buy products that they do not really need because they feel empty and unhappy. For instance, people often consume alcohol, cigarettes or sugary foods because these enhance mood. Indeed, the link between emotion and buying is evident in the fact that much of the content of advertisements has little to do with giving factual information about the product being promoted.

2 People often buy products they do not really need because they want to display their status or wealth. A good example of this is when people dispose of perfectly good items (clothing, furniture, electronic goods) simply to buy a more up-to-date model. Another example is when shoppers choose high-value brands that prominently display their logos over anonymous brands that are equivalent in quality but cheaper. Indeed, the relationship between social status and consumer spending is so powerful that many brands are carefully targeted at particular social groups.

3 Sometimes people buy products they do not really need because they want to use them in a positive way to make their lives more enjoyable or interesting. In an ideal world, all people would have some disposable income with which to buy products or services that enhance their lives in some way. Hobbies, music and novels, for example, are all products that are not strictly necessary for survival but can contribute greatly to quality of life.

Exercise 8

(Suggested answer)

It is likely that financial institutions are at least partially responsible for high levels of personal debt. In times when lenders are less tightly regulated and greater competition is allowed, there is a natural tendency to try to attract more customers by making it easier to borrow money. Banks may choose to lend to people who have relatively low incomes or who already have high levels of personal debt. This practice may be sustainable up to a point; however, when the economy suffers and people lose their jobs, the situation can quickly reach a crisis point, as has been clearly shown in the recession experienced by many countries in recent years.

Part 3: Exam practice

Task 1: Model answer

The line graph shows economic growth over a 15-year period ending in 2020. The pie charts give a breakdown of household spending in four separate years over the same period. Viewed together, there appears to be a relationship between economic growth and patterns of spending.

According to the graph, economic growth began at a modest 1%, rose slightly, then remained more or less steady at about 2% until 2013. It grew sharply and peaked at nearly 5% in 2015, then fell dramatically to –5% in 2018, before recovering to 1% in 2020.

Over the same period, changes in patterns of spending were evident. In periods of low or negative growth, spending on housing and food accounted for a larger proportion of total household expenditure than in times of relative prosperity. This is particularly evident in the chart for 2020 where together these three items appear to account for 65-70% of total expenditure. Conversely, in times of economic growth, spending on less essential items such as travel, entertainment and clothing tended to increase.

In summary, the figures show that in times of hardship, households spend a greater proportion of their income on necessities whereas, in times of prosperity, more is spent on non-essentials.

[202 words]

Task 2: Model answer

Learning to manage money is something that virtually everyone must do as the ability to maintain a balance between income and expenditure is essential for a stable life. In many developed countries, the availability of easy credit and a wide variety of financial products has made the task of managing one's money more complex. In less affluent parts of the world, lack of money or access to credit creates its own challenges. In this essay, I will outline two ways in which people can learn to manage their money.

Learning by example is one important method. From their early years, children can observe how their parents make financial decisions. They may notice, for example, whether money is saved for costly purchases, or whether purchases are bought on credit. Children can also see what kinds of criteria parents use when choosing what to buy, for instance, whether quality of quantity is more important. It is important, therefore, that parents model sensible purchasing behaviour and explain what they are doing and why. However, in many circumstances, this may not be enough.

Another important means of teaching people to manage money is through education. When school children, for instance, learn arithmetic, they could also be taught the basics of budgeting and how to recognise good value. For adults, the Internet could be a good source of advice on how to save money. Price comparison websites, for example, can be a good way of researching what is available before making an expensive purchase.

The ability to manage money is often taken for granted. Because the consequences of poor money management can be severe, it is worthwhile taking steps to ensure people are as well-informed as possible.

[282 words]

Exam tutor

1 food and drink, transportation, clothing and footwear, entertainment, housing, dining out, utilities, home furnishings, furniture, electronic goods, jewellery, children's toys, sportswear.
2 In IELTS Writing you should avoid vague words and try to use precise expressions.
3 You can describe visual prompts separately, but normally you should indicate how they are related.
4 *when ... rise(s), ... also appear(s) to ...; when ... fall(s), ... appear(s) to ...; the less ... the more ...; the more ... the more ...* .
5 To signpost examples: *for example, an example of this is ..., for instance;* to reinforce a main point: *indeed, in fact.*

Unit 8

Part 1: Language development

Expressions related to age

Exercise 1
5 c   2 e   3 b   4 a   1 d
(From youngest to oldest): infancy, childhood, adolescence, adulthood, old age

Rights and responsibilities expressions

Exercise 2
Rights: a, d, f, g, h
Responsibilities: b, c, e, i, j

Exercise 3
1 forced   2 empowered   3 compelled   4 have a duty to do
5 coerced into joining

Exercise 4
1 over   2 in   3 with; on   4 with   5 of   6 of; into   7 from for   8 in; of

Exercise 5
1 in the best interests   2 taken into account   3 cooperate with others   4 interfering too much in their lives   5 exercise too much control over

Part 2: Exam skills

Task 1: Developing a paragraph with supporting details

Exercise 1

1 Response 2 is more satisfactory because it includes examples from the table to support the main point.

2 The writer wants to emphasise the difference in opinion between parents and adolescents, so he/she has chosen those details that illustrate the biggest gap in views.

Signaling supporting details

Exercise 2

1 the most common   2 for instance, such as   3 in particular, particularly   4 the sole

Exercise 3

> Overall, parents said that they wanted significantly more control over their children than did the adolescents surveyed. This is <u>particularly</u> (3) evident in the issue of 'how adolescents spend their free time' and 'what friends they make'. Roughly three out of four parents wanted to place restrictions on these areas, whereas only one in five children felt this was needed. The <u>biggest</u> (1) conflict of opinion concerned young people's choice of friends, with nearly 80 percent of mothers believing they should exercise control and only 17 percent of adolescent girls agreeing. The <u>only</u> (4) area where there was some agreement among parents and young people was in restrictions on choice of subjects for study, selected by 58 percent of mothers and 49 percent of adolescent boys.

Exercise 4

1 only (or sole)   2 particularly (or most)   3 biggest (or widest)

Exercise 5

(Suggested answer)

The adolescent boys surveyed also indicated a greater acceptance of parental control than did the adolescent girls. The two areas where girls accepted greater control were how they spend their free time and how they spend their money. The biggest gap between boys and girls was over what subject they study. Forty-nine percent of boys said they agreed with parental restrictions in this area, whereas only a third of girls felt this was needed.

Task 2: Using modal verbs appropriately

Exercise 6

a 2   b 5, 8   c 1   d 3, 6   e 4, 7, 9

Exercise 7

1 *can*, *could* and *would* because this Task 2 question asks you to make suggestions and *would* is used to explain the possible consequences.

2 *should* is a less emphatic term than *must* and is used to express necessity.

3 *may* is used to express a possibility or permission.

Exercise 8

1 would
2 may / might
3 should / must
4 can / could
5 can / could
6 would
7 might / may / could
8 can / could
9 would
10 could / would

Developing a conclusion

Exercise 9

1 c   2 d   3 a   4 b   5 d

Exercise 10

1 In short
2 In brief, In summary, In conclusion
3 a
4 d
5 Society can ensure that children's rights are taken into account, that children have access to help, and that children are properly informed of their rights.

Exercise 11

(Suggested answer)

In summary, there are several ways in which young people can be encouraged to behave responsibly. They can be involved in defining what constitutes good behaviour, and they can be taught leadership skills. Parents and teachers should be encouraged to try these methods before resorting to more punitive measures. If they are successful, they may very well discover a maturity in their children that they never anticipated.

Part 3: Exam practice

Task 1: Model answer

The bar chart illustrates the views of 1000 young people in five countries around the world on the most suitable age for three key rights and responsibilities to be given to young people.

There was some variation in the views of all five nationalities for all three categories. For marriage, the minimum age identified ranged from a low of 16 in Egypt and Mexico to a high of 22 in Japan. Respondents in the UK and the US chose 18.

A similar pattern was seen in the results concerning voting age. Again, this was highest among the Japanese participants and lowest (16) among those in Mexico and the UK.

Interestingly, for all of the countries surveyed, the participants set their preferred age of criminal responsibility at a lower point than either of the rights. The gap was particularly wide in the US, where respondents identified 12 as the age at which children should be held responsible for their crimes.

Overall, the results show that adolescents in different countries have different views of when it is appropriate for young people to hold certain responsibilities associated with adulthood.

[186 words]

Task 2: Model answer

As children grow up, they can be increasingly responsible for making their own decisions. However, until a young person is ready to live independently, parents still have a responsibility for guiding their children. In this essay, I will outline two main areas in which I believe parents should continue to exercise some control over their adolescent children.

The most important area is safety. Learning to manage risk is clearly very important. However, because children often have less experience of, and therefore less awareness of, adverse consequences, they are not always able to take sensible precautions. Because, for example, they may never have been robbed whilst outdoors at night, they may assume that this can never happen to them. Parents should therefore intervene to help their children understand and manage risk. In the example above, they could help their child arrange suitable transport.

Another area in which a degree of parental intervention is necessary is in considering long-term interests. Young people sometimes have a tendency to prioritise short-term needs and wants over longer-term goals. They may, for instance, choose to attend a sporting event or social occasion rather than study for an exam that is weeks in the future. Parents can help their children by insisting that certain responsibilities are met before privileges are granted. Children would not only be helped to achieve their goals but would also learn how to manage their time.

In summary, parents should allow their adolescent children a degree of autonomy but continue to exercise some control. If they intervene with a view to helping their child learn to make good decisions independently, they are likely to see the best outcome.

[275 words]

Exam tutor

1 *be entitled to, be empowered to, be allowed to, to be authorised to, be permitted to*
2 superlatives, expressions indicating example, focusing expressions, expressions indicating uniqueness.
3 Modal verbs are commonly used with other verbs to indicate intention, obligation, permission, ability and possibility.
4 *Can* is used to express permission (e.g. *Children can leave school at the age of 16*), ability (e.g. *Most children van read by the age of six.*), and possibility (e.g. *Too much parental control can cause children to rebel.*)
5 restate your opinion, summarise the main points, make a recommendation, make a prediction.

Unit 9

Part 1: Language development

Expressions related to people and places

Exercise 1
1 density   2 accelerate   3 census   4 demographic
5 elderly   6 boom   7 generation

Exercise 2
Causes: b, c, f, h   Consequences: a, d, e, g

Exercise 3
1 growing pressure on care givers
2 Dwindling pension funds

3 Improved health care
4 Decreasing mortality from infectious diseases
5 increasing incidence of chronic illnesses
6 increasing public health costs
7 Family planning

Cohesive devices

Exercise 4
1 b   2 d   3 a   4 c   5 e

Part 2: Exam skills:

Task 1: Correcting punctuation

Exercise 1

> Many people enjoy retirement. **They** find they have the time for activities they enjoy.
>
> Lower mortality is due to increased longevity, **which** results from improved health care.
>
> There are more jobs opportunities in cities, **so** people migrate to them from rural areas.
>
> **Because** couples are under pressure to work, they often delay starting a family.
>
> People want to enjoy retirement; **however**, they do not always save enough for a comfortable retirement.

1 Use a comma before the coordinating conjunction.
2 Use a semicolon before the conjunctive adverb, or a full stop, e.g. … *retirement. However, they do not always* …
3 Use a comma when the relative clause gives extra information; if the relative clause defines the subject don't use a comma, e.g. *Only people who retire at 65 can receive a pension.*
4 Use a comma when the clause with the subordinating conjunction comes first. If the subordinate clause comes after the main clause, you don't need a comma, e.g. *Couples often delay starting a family because they are under pressure to work.*

Exercise 2

The graph illustrates two contrasting trends. Whereas the proportion of the world's population aged 65 and above is expected to rise, the proportion of those under five is expected to decline. The proportion of elderly people has risen gradually from approximately 5% in 1950 to roughly 7.5% today, and over the next 30 years it is expected to more than double. However, the proportion of young children has fallen gradually since 1970 from approximately 14% to 9%. It is forecast to continue falling at roughly the same rate until 2040, when it will level off.

Improving a paragraph by combining sentences

Exercise 3

(Suggested answers)

1 The bar chart shows the percentage of males and females who were over the age of 65 in 2000.
2 Korea, Mexico, and Turkey are all developing or newly industrialized countries which are expected to experience large increases in the proportion of the population that is elderly.
3 The biggest increase is likely to occur in Korea, where the proportion of pensioners is expected to increase from 10% to 35%.
4 The changes in all three countries will occur from a relatively low base, so the predicted proportion of elderly residents will still be lower than that expected in developed economies.

Removing unnecessary words

Exercise 4

(Suggested answer)

The figure shows the distribution of the population in terms of gender and age. The age group with the highest percentage of both men and women is 55 to 59. Roughly five percent of the population is in this age group. The age groups with the next highest proportion of the population are 30 to 34 and 35 to 39. Interestingly, until the age of 59, the proportion of males and females is roughly equal. However, thereafter, women make up a higher proportion of the elderly population. This trend is particularly evident in those aged 80 plus. Over four percent of women fall into in this category, whereas only two percent of men have reached this age.

Task 2: Creating cohesion with summary words

Exercise 5

(Suggested answers)
1 development / shift
2 concerns / disadvantages / drawbacks
3 strategy / measure / approach
4 process

Exercise 6

1 The last sentence of the introduction. This is often referred to as the thesis statement: *A number of measures can be taken to ensure that the elderly can enjoy life after retirement.*
2 *measure*
3 *measure* occurs in the first (topic) sentence of each of the following two body paragraphs
4 *older people, the elderly, elderly people, all, increasingly frail section of the population*
5 *sums of money, savings*

Repetition and synonyms

Exercise 7

(Suggested answers)
1 Synonyms for *younger family members* could include: *the younger generation, younger relatives, younger relations, younger members of the family*
Synonyms for *older relations* could include: *the older generation, older family members, older relations, elderly relatives, senior members of the family*

Exercise 8

In most societies, adults in their prime are expected to care for those who are becoming frailer due to old age. How one defines the specific responsibilities of younger family members towards older relations, however, depends on a number of factors, for example, the family's resources and the degree of state support available. Nevertheless, I would suggest a number of core obligations can be identified.

Exercise 9

1 Circle *arguments*; underline <u>mandatory retirement age</u>

2 Circle *consequences*; underline <u>population ageing</u>

Topic sentences

Exercise 10

1 <u>The most fundamental obligation</u> that younger family members have towards older relations is to ensure that their (physical needs) are being met.

2 <u>Another core obligation</u> is to ensure that older relations continue to feel a sense of (love and belonging)

3 Finally, <u>younger family members should ensure that older relations continue to have the opportunity to grow and develop</u> (as individuals)

Exercise 11

(Suggested topic sentences)

1 One of the main consequences of population ageing is the increasing incidence of illnesses and ailments commonly associated with age.

2 Another consequence is growing pressure on care givers, often sons and daughters who may themselves be in the process of raising a family of their own.

3 A final consequence is pressure on pension funds.

(Suggested paragraph)

> One of the main consequences of population ageing is the increasing incidence of illnesses and ailments commonly associated with age. Cancer, heart disease, and arthritis, for example, are all on the rise in many countries with ageing populations. This trend can result in pressure on health budgets and services.

Part 3: Exam practice

Task 1: Model answer

> The line graph shows three demographic trends between 1940 and 2010: birth rate, population growth rate, and death rate.
>
> The birth rate followed a falling trend overall from 2.5% in 1940 to a 0.5 rise in 2020. There were brief increases in the late 1940s and 1960s followed by more substantial falls, particularly between 1950 and 1960.
>
> The population growth rate followed a very similar trend with a brief time lag, suggesting a strong link between birth rate and population rate. The main difference in the two trends was a more substantial rise in population growth between 1945 and 1955.
>
> The death rate showed a somewhat different trend. There was a steady fall between 1940 and 1955, followed by a very gradual decline over the next 45 years. There was a slight rise over the next decade, presumably as the 'boom' generation of 75 years previously reached the end of its life span.
>
> Overall, the trends show a declining population.
>
> **[160 words]**

Task 2: Model answer

People today can expect to live a longer and healthier life than people in the past. People often see retirement as a time for relaxation and letting go of the stresses of working life. However, many who reach retirement age are more interested than ever in contributing actively to their communities. This essay will outline two ways in which this interest can benefit society.

Becoming involved in schools is one of the ways in which the life experience of the elderly can be made available to the community. Because families now are often more mobile than in the past, many children do not have regular contact with grandparents. Yet children are often fascinated by stories of life in the past. Inviting local retired people into schools to speak to children can help to maintain a vital link between past and present.

Another way in which society can benefit from a more active older generation is by inviting older employees to remain in work part-time. Older people may not want to or indeed be able to do a full day's work; however, their experience may continue to be valuable to their employers. A good example of this can be seen in one scheme in the UK in which elder employees remained in work as mentors for younger employees.

Schools and the workplace are just two of the areas in which those who have reached retirement age can continue to contribute to their communities. As life expectancy improves, the need to maintain an active and socially meaningful life may also increase. Experience suggests that this trend can have benefits for all, not just the elderly.

[273 words]

Exam tutor

1 People know they are going to grow older, but they often do not prepare adequately for old age.
   Although people know they are going to grow older, they often do not prepare adequately for old age.
   People know they are going to grow older; however, they often do not prepare adequately for old age.
2 It is more important to use words such as *however* to signal contrasting ideas than to use words like *moreover* to signal additional points because the reader will normally expect each new point to reinforce the previous point unless the writer has indicated otherwise.
3 The thesis statement is usually placed towards the end of the introduction.
4 Each topic sentence advances the main idea expressed in the thesis statement.
5 Repeating a key word or phrase from the thesis statement or exam question makes the connection between each point and the main topic of the essay more obvious.

Unit 10

Part 1: Language development
Expressions related to popular culture

Exercise 1
1 e 2 f 3 c 4 h 5 b 6 a 7 d 8 i 9 g

Exercise 2
1 impression 2 aspirations 3 image 4 fame
5 flawed 6 icon

Exercise 3
1 well-known / famous / legendary
2 imperfect / bad / worthless
3 like / admire / idolize
4 recognition / praise / acclaim
5 fleeting / transient / brief

Expressing attitude with adverbs

Exercise 4
1 Unfortunately … 2 Inevitably … 3 Fortunately …
4 Surprisingly … 5 Obviously … 6 Interestingly …
7 Importantly …

Modifying adverbs

Exercise 5
1 Less obviously … 2 More importantly …
3 Not surprisingly … 4 Somewhat surprisingly …

Part 2: Exam skills

Task 1: Commonly confused words

Exercise 1
1 past   2 except   3 rose   4 than   5 in contrast   6 feature

Exercise 2
1 rose   2 than   3 past   4 feature   5 except

Using formal language

Exercise 3
1 significant   2 Many   3 For example   4 Surprisingly
5 did not   6 appear

Synonyms to avoid repetition

Exercise 4
1 featured   2 occupations   3 those surveyed   4 selecting
5 career   6 occupied

Exercise 5
1 receiving   2 percentage   3 negative   4 small   5 On the
other hand   6 was not   7 there appears to be
Underlined expressions: those surveyed, people questioned,
those who took part in the survey, survey respondents

Task 2: Choosing the right level of formality

Exercise 6

Suggested answers
1 benefit, positive consequence   2 drawback, negative
consequence   3 view, point of view   4 nevertheless
5 individuals   6 dilemma, difficulty   7 approach, strategy   8
significant, noteworthy   9 topic, concern
10 circumstances, context

Exercise 7
1 Paragraph c is the best.
2 Paragraph a is too informal; paragraph b is too emphatic in
   tone; paragraph d has too much repetition.

Exercise 8

> In the past, people (1) *generally* became famous for **their achievements**. Einstein, Dickens, and Gandhi, for instance, were all celebrated for **their contributions** to science, literature, and public life. People were interested in them (2) *primarily* because they were role models.
> One of the reasons fame today is so different is because celebrities (3) *appear to* satisfy a range of people's emotional needs, not just the need for role models. **Many** celebrities today are famous simply for being famous. The public are (4) *often* interested in them because, when news of scandals **emerges**, they (5) *can experience* the satisfaction of feeling superior to people they envy.

Exercise 9

(Suggested answer)

> Another reason fame today is unique is the desire for ordinary people to explore the nature of fame itself. Many celebrities that have achieved fame through the Internet, for example, come from the same backgrounds as **the viewing public**. Watching **such people** allow **ordinary individuals** to imagine what it might be like to suddenly find themselves in the public eye. **People who are famous for being famou**s may, therefore, allow **unremarkable people** to enjoy wish fulfillment fantasies without having to worry about whether they are capable of significant achievement.
>
> The third, and perhaps most significant reason that celebrities play such an important role in modern life is the fact that commercial pressures encourage media organisations to focus on information that is immediately attractive to **the consumer**. As we have seen, the *'**cult of celebrity**'* appears to tap into powerful emotional needs: the need to feel superior, the need to imagine oneself to be the centre of attention; therefore, **celebrity news** sells.

Part 3: Exam practice

Task 1: Model answer

The table gives the results of an opinion poll in which respondents were asked about their views of celebrity news coverage.

There were clear majority views for all three questions asked. The vast majority of those questioned (85%), for example, said that there was too much news coverage of celebrities. Only 7% said there was the right amount, and an even smaller percentage (6%) said there was too little.

The public was somewhat more divided on the question of who was responsible for the quantity of celebrity news. A majority (56%) said the news organisations were; However, over a third felt that the public were at fault. Roughly one in ten respondents felt that both were responsible.

When asked to identify the news medium responsible for providing most of the coverage, most of those polled singled out online news websites. Television news programmes were identified by 15% of respondents, followed by newspapers (12%).

Overall, the findings suggest that most people think there is too much focus on celebrities in the news and that online news websites are largely to blame.

[180 words]

Task 2: Model answer

In the past, news about famous people may have been confined to gossip columns in newspapers; these days it is not uncommon for celebrities to feature as front-page news. There is evidence that the public feels there is too much news coverage of famous people. Not surprisingly, there is concern about how this might be affecting people, and in particular children.

One of the possible negative consequences of the 'cult of celebrity' is the tendency to confuse fame and notoriety. Celebrity scandals are just as likely to receive publicity as celebrity achievements. Indeed, some famous people have received more attention for their misuse of drugs and alcohol than for their successes on the stage or in sports. Children who crave attention may come to see misbehaviour as normal.

The emphasis on individuals in the public eye may also be at the expense of serious news coverage. Next to the superficial excitement of celebrity gossip, news about serious events and issues that have a more profound effect on people's lives may seem uninteresting. Children may be forming a very distorted picture of how the world works.

The negative influence of celebrities on children can also be seen in children's career aspirations. These days, young people are much more likely to see themselves as potential sports stars or entertainers. The prevalence of these figures in the mass media may convey the impression that such positions are plentiful. Children may be developing unrealistic expectations that they too will become rich and famous.

In summary, the 'cult of celebrity' may be affecting children in a number of undesirable ways. It is important that children be taught to critically evaluate what they see in the media so that they can form a more realistic view of society, acceptable behaviour, and indeed themselves.

[297 words]

Exam tutor

1 Use attitude adverbs e.g. *fortunately, unfortunately, importantly, inevitably, interestingly, obviously, surprisingly.*
2 Because many words that look or sound similar may have very different meanings.
3 Issues of general interest, people and opinions, problems and solutions, advantages and disadvantages.
4 Academic style is often more cautious and modest than everyday speech.
5 Use hedging expressions, e.g. adverbs such as *generally, primarily often,* verbs such as *appear,* modal verbs such as *can.*

Unit 11

Part 1: Language development
Expressions associated with transport

Exercise 1
1 d   2 a   3 h   4 e 5 g   6 f 7 b 8 c

Exercise 2
1 cycle routes   2 speed cameras   3 pedestrians / danger
4 traffic congestion   5 motorways   6 road works
7 bus lanes

Word formation and parts of speech

Exercise 3

verb	noun
reduce	reduction
produce	production
convert	**conversion**
maintain	**maintenance**
emit	emission
combust	**combustion**
propel	**propulsion**

Exercise 4
1 propelled 2 converting   3 propulsion   4 reduce
5 combustion 6 emissions   7 emit   8 maintenance
9 produce   10 production

Exercise 5
a achievement   b appearance   c allowance   d explanation   e involvement   f provision   g opposition

Exercise 6
1 opposition   2 achievement   3 explanation   4 appearance   5 provision   6 allowances   7 involvement

Part 2: Exam skills

Task 1: Correcting errors in verb forms and articles

Exercise 1
1 was 2 have risen 3 continues 4 correlates 5 increased
6 was already rising / had already risen

Exercise 2
1 decreased 2 are expected 3 correlates 4 varied
5 accounted 6 were asked

Exercise 3
1 driving 2 to use 3 purchasing 4 change 5 travelling
6 to reduce

Exercise 4
1 d 2 e 3 c 4 a 5 b

Exercise 5
1 The 2 - 3 - 4 the 5 - 6 the 7 the 8 the 9 a
10 a 11 the

Task 2: Correcting errors in sentence structure

Exercise 6
a 9 b 2 c 1 d 5 e 4 f 7 g 6 h 3 i 8 j 10

1 The **evidence shows** that wearing a seatbelt significantly reduces road accident fatalities. (countable vs. uncountable noun)
2 In fact wearing a seatbelt is **the** most important safety measure that can be taken. (use of the article)
3 The number of road accidents **declined** last year. (tense)
4 It is **illegal** to drive without a license or car insurance. (word class)
5 The cost of insurance depends **on** several factors including age, experience and type of car. (preposition)
6 Organisations such as the AA **can provide** assistance to motorists who break down. (verb form)
7 Many people **who** live in rural areas have no choice but to travel by car. (relative clause)
8 Buying a second-hand car is sometimes **risky**. **Inexperienced** buyers can be easily cheated. (run-on sentence)

9 There **are** numerous examples of illegal practices in the second-hand motor trade. (subject-verb agreement)
10 **This is because** the industry is poorly regulated and buyers are not always well-informed. (sentence fragment)

Exercise 7
1 As people in many parts of the world now have greater access to cars, they often have more choice over where they live and work.
2 Cities have become more sprawling because people have sought out the greater privacy and space afforded by suburban living.
3 There are more vehicles, often travelling at greater speed; as a consequence, the streets are less hospitable to pedestrians.
4 There has also been a decline in public transport; as a result, people have less day-to-day contact with other members of their community.
5 Since most people are very dependent on their cars, they do not want to give them up.

Punctuation and linking

Exercise 8
1 Although most people say they would use other forms of transport for short journeys, in fact, most car journeys are for distances of less than two miles.
2 Most people are reluctant to buy electric cars because of three main factors: cost, maintenance and reliability.
3 Some of those surveyed said they had concerns about the distance electric cars could travel before having to be recharged.
4 Electric cars are more expensive than conventional cars. However, their maintenance costs are lower.
5 One major Japanese car manufacturer, which produces some of the most fuel-efficient petrol-powered cars, has recently announced that it plans to invest more heavily in electric car technology.
6 Hybrid and electric cars produce fewer emissions, but this may not result in a reduction in overall emissions because the growth in car ownership over the next 15 years is likely to accelerate.

Exercise 9

In many parts of the world, people now have greater access to cars. **Therefore**, they often have more choice over where they live and work. Cities have become more sprawling, **as** people have sought out the greater privacy and space afforded by suburban living. **Because** there are more vehicles, often travelling at greater speed, the streets are less hospitable to pedestrians. There has also been a decline in public transport. **As a consequence,** people have less day-to-day contact with other members of their community.

Proofreading your work

Exercise 10

One of the factors that distinguishes developed from developing economies is mass car ownership. ~~The~~ Cars undoubtedly have practical benefits for the individuals who own them. They allow for more flexible and autonomous travel. Like other consumer items, they can **be** used to express individual taste and identity**. However,** they also clearly have a number of undesirable consequences.

One of these consequences is **deterioration** in people's health. Urban pollution, which is largely caused by vehicle emissions, can exacerbate respiratory problems such as asthma. These health problems are more prevalent in cities, particularly among children and **the** elderly.

Another consequence of car use is a decline in levels of physical activity and hence levels of fitness. Although this is partly a consequence of rising prosperity generally**,** there is **evidence** that car use is responsible for lower levels of cardiovascular fitness. The vast majority of car journeys are for less than two miles, that is, distances that can easily be covered on foot. In short, when **the** people own cars, they tend to **walk** less, thus removing a major means by which people maintain day-to-day fitness.

Part 3: Exam practice

Task 1: Model answer

The table compares modes of transport used in four countries: the USA, the UK, France and the Netherlands. Percentages of journeys made by car, bicycle, public transport and on foot are given. The bar chart shows the results of a survey into reasons people in the USA travel to work by car.

As can be seen from the table, cars were the most frequently used form of transport in all four countries. However, the proportion of journeys made by car ranged from a low of 47% in the Netherlands to a high of 90% in the USA. Figures for the other forms of transport also varied considerably. Not surprisingly, in the Netherlands, a high proportion of trips were made by bicycle (26%) and on foot (18%). The highest rate of public transport use was in France, where nearly one in five journeys was made by public transport.

The bar chart provides information that may help explain why car use is so high in the USA. The most frequently cited reason was lack of any other alternative (38%). Although a sizable percentage said it was more convenient (21%), the other factors listed appeared to relate more to need than preference, e.g. working night shift.

Overall, the figures show considerable variation in modes of transport used, though the car continues to dominate in most contexts.

[223 words]

Task 2: Model answer

Mass car ownership clearly has a number of undesirable consequences for people's health and fitness as well as for the environment and community life generally. Nevertheless, owning a car is still seen as a desirable option. In fact, there are more than a billion cars in the world today and that number is growing. Although this trend may seem inexorable, there is much that can be done to discourage unnecessary car use.

One possible approach is to make cars expensive to own and use, for example, by taxing them at the point of purchase or annually through a road tax. Certain types of car use, for instance short journeys within already congested cities, can also be discouraged through road pricing schemes such as that operating in London. However, these punitive measures alone are unlikely to have a major impact unless alternative means of transport are available.

Evidence suggests that where public transport options are plentiful, convenient and reliable, people will use them. Inhabitants of cities such as Paris, which have invested heavily in commuter rail networks, are more likely to use public transport than people living in cities where such networks have been allowed to deteriorate.

A less expensive and more environmentally sound option is to create a network of cycle lanes and other facilities for cyclists, such as safe weather-proof shelters for parking bicycles. This has the additional advantage of encouraging people to keep fit whilst allowing them the flexibility of autonomous travel. Cities in the Netherlands, which have relatively high rates of cycling, have shown how this can work.

In brief, the trend towards rising car ownership and use need not be inexorable. People can be encouraged to use other means of transport. However, rhetoric alone is unlikely to bring about change. Investment in practical alternatives is what is needed above all.

[304 words]

Exam tutor

1 You should spend approximately 20 minutes on Task 1 and 40 minutes on Task 2. Remember to leave a few minutes at the end to check your work for errors.
2 You should write at least 150 words for Task 1 and 250 words for Task 2. Remember, you will not get extra points if you write more.
3 A Task 1 prompt could be a line graph, bar chart, pie chart, table, diagram, map, or a combination of these.
4 Task 2 essay questions usually require you to do one of the following: propose one or more solutions to a problem, evaluate a solution to a problem, provide an explanation or prediction, evaluate an idea or belief.
5 Your writing will be assessed against four criteria: task achievement (how well you have answered the question), coherence and cohesion (logical flow of ideas information), lexical resource (your knowledge of vocabulary), and grammatical range and accuracy (accurate use of a range of different structures).

12: Practice exam

Task 1: Model answer

The chart shows the percentage of the population engaging in the seven most common leisure activities on a weekly basis in 2015 and in 2019.

The two most popular activities were watching television and having a meal together as a family. These were also the only two activities that increased in popularity over the five-year period. Watching TV went up from 90 to 92 percent. Eating together also increased by two percentage points to 77 percent.

The next most common leisure pursuits were, like watching TV, all screen-based: watching films (enjoyed by nearly half the population), watching sport, and playing computer games (enjoyed by just over a third of people). However, the popularity of these pursuits all decreased by two to percent.

The final two activities represented in the chart both involved going out of the house. Both of these declined more sharply. Going out shopping fell from 33 to 30 percent, while going out to a café fell by seven percentage points to 25 percent.

Overall, the chart shows that indoor pursuits were most popular and some increasingly so, whereas activities outside of the home were less popular and in fact declined in popularity.

[199 words]

Task 2: Model answer

The issue of equality and achievement has occupied people throughout history. Some argue that because people vary in terms of talent and initiative, inequality is inevitable. The job of the government is to ensure freedom for each to achieve his or her personal best. Others believe that because wealth and therefore opportunity tend to concentrate in the hands of a few, the government must actively redistribute resources. While I believe there is some truth in both views, the latter is likely to yield greater life satisfaction for the majority.

Societies that are very unequal in terms of income and resources are often credited with great achievements. The United States, for example, has many successful individuals in business and science. Its universities, among the world's most expensive, rank among the top ten in the world and employ a disproportionately large number of Nobel-prize winners. However, such countries also often produce many people without qualifications, and poor prospects.

More egalitarian countries often achieve higher average rates of success. Finland and Korea, for example, which invest heavily in free public education for all, tend to rank high in international comparisons of literacy and numeracy rates. Although such countries do not always produce many internationally successful 'superstars', they tend to have a high proportion of moderately successful people in terms of employment and income. More importantly, they have lower rates of absolute deprivation and underachievement.

In short, if we allow freedom for individuals to achieve their potential, some inequality is inevitable. However, success usually generates wealth, which can be passed from one generation to another resulting in inequality of opportunity regardless of individual merit. It therefore, makes sense for society to level the playing field.

[281 words]

Sample IELTS Writing answer sheets

IELTS Writing Answer Sheet - TASK 1

Candidate Name

Candidate No.

Centre No.

Test Module ☐ Academic ☐ General Training

Test Date Day Month Year

If you need more space to write your answer, use an additional sheet and write in the space provided to indicate how many sheets you are using: Sheet of

Writing   Task 1   Writing   Task 1   Writing   Task 1   Writing   Task 1

Sample Answer Sheet

Do not write below this line

Do not write in this area. Please continue your answer on the other side of this sheet.

23505

IELTS Writing Answer Sheet - TASK 2

Candidate Name	

Candidate No.						Centre No.					

Test Module	☐ Academic ☐ General Training	Test Date	Day		Month		Year			

If you need more space to write your answer, use an additional sheet and write in the space provided to indicate how many sheets you are using: Sheet ☐ of ☐

Writing   Task 2   Writing   Task 2   Writing   Task 2   Writing   Task 2

Sample Answer Sheet

Do not write below this line

Do not write in this area. Please continue your answer on the other side of this sheet.

39507

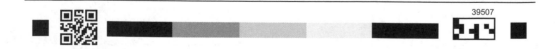